Iraq
in a nutshell

*

Enisen Publishing

*Iraq's flag adopted on July 31, 1963 had three bands of red, white and black (the color scheme used by neighboring Arab nations) with three green 5-pointed stars. The stars originally symbolized the unity between Iraq, Egypt and Syria within the proposed United Arab Republic (UAR). When the UAR was dissolved, the stars came to represent the three tenets of the Baathist party – Unity, Freedom and Socialism.

During the 1991 Gulf War, Saddam Hussein added the Arabic words "*Allahu akbar*" ("God is great") to give the flag, and his regime, a more Islamic appearance. The script, believed to have been written in Saddam's own handwriting, was replaced with a more stylized Arabic Kufic script in mid-2004. The stars were removed in January 2008.

Note: This book uses the initials B.C. ("before Christ") and A.D. ("Anno Domini," or "in the year of our Lord") rather than B.C.E. ("Before the Common Era") and C.E. (in the Common Era") to designate time periods since the writer and editors felt the former terms were more familiar to Nutshell Notes readers.

First published – March 2003
First edition – March 2003
Second edition – September 2004
Third edition – January 2008
Fourth edition – October 2011

Enisen Publishing
2118 Wilshire Boulevard, #351
Santa Monica, CA 90403-5784
www.enisen.com
publishing@enisen.com

Text   Amanda Roraback
Maps   Katie Gerber
Editor-in-Chief D.A. Roraback
Editor   Kal Rubaye

Copyright © 2003, 2004, 2008, 2011 by Enisen Publishing and Nutshell Notes, LLC

All rights reserved. No part of this book may be reproduced in any form or by any means without written permission from Enisen Publishing.

Nutshell Notes and the Nutshell Notes logo are trademarks of Enisen Publishing and Nutshell Notes, LLC.

ISBN: 978-0-9763070-3-7

Printed in the United States of America

Table of Contents

FACTS AND FIGURES — 1
ANCIENT HISTORY — 2
INTRODUCTION OF ISLAM — 13
EUROPEAN INTERFERENCE — 20
SADDAM HUSSEIN — 27
IRAN-IRAQ WAR — 30
GULF WAR — 33
NEOCONS — 39
ARGUMENTS IN FAVOR OF WAR (2003) — 42
ARGUMENTS AGAINST WAR (2003) — 43
OPERATION IRAQI FREEDOM — 44
POST-SADDAM GOVERNMENTS — 49
POLITICAL PARTIES — 59
IRAQ'S CONSTITUTION — 61
KURDS — 63
MARSH ARABS — 71
TURKMEN (TURKOMAN) — 72
ASSYRIANS — 73
SHI'ITES (SHI'AS) — 74
SHI'A TERMS — 78
SHI'ITE (SHI'A) MOVEMENTS — 81
SUNNI INSURGENCY — 87
U.S. WITHDRAWAL FROM IRAQ — 93
MAJOR ISSUES — 95
THE POLITICS OF OIL — 102
WEAPONS OF MASS DESTRUCTION (WMDs) — 106
UN RESOLUTIONS — 111
IRAQ STUDY GROUP REPORT — 114

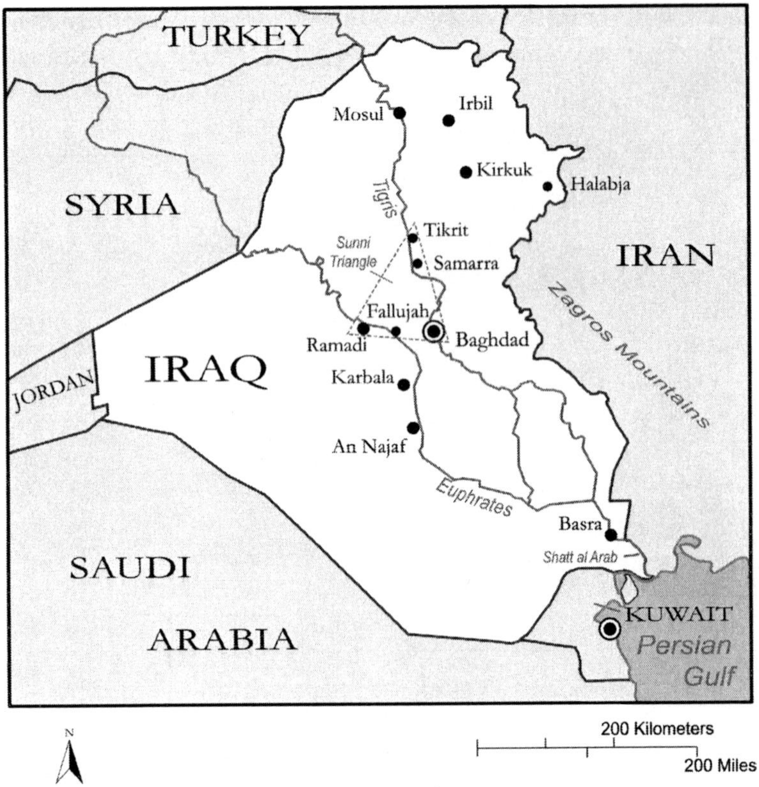
TURKEY
SYRIA
IRAN
IRAQ
JORDAN
SAUDI
ARABIA
KUWAIT
Persian
Gulf
Mosul
Irbil
Kirkuk
Halabja
Tigris
Tikrit
Sunni
Triangle
Samarra
Zagros Mountains
Fallujah
Ramadi
Baghdad
Karbala
An Najaf
Euphrates
Basra
Shatt al Arab
N
200 Kilometers
200 Miles

Black Sea
BULGARIA
GEORGIA
Caspian
Sea
ARM.
AZER.
TURKEY
TURKMENISTAN
Mediterranean
Sea
SYRIA
LEBANON
ISRAEL
JORDAN
IRAQ
IRAN
AFGH.
Persian Gulf
PAK.
EGYPT
SAUDI
ARABIA
OMAN
Red Sea
SUDAN
Arabian Sea
ERITREA
YEMEN

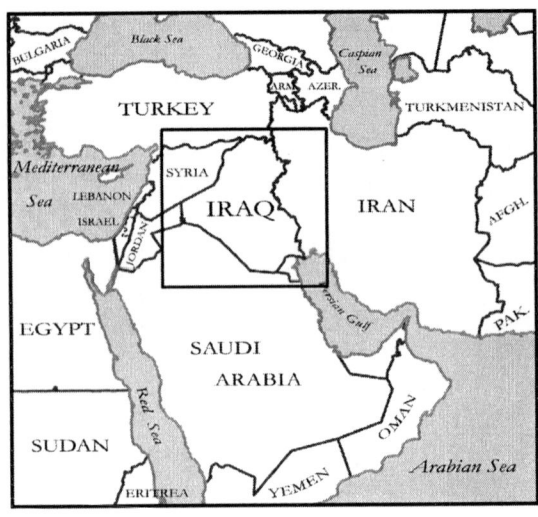

Iraq in a Nutshell

FACTS AND FIGURES

Country Name: Republic of Iraq

Local Long Form: Jumhuriyah al Iraq; Local Short Form: Al Iraq

Government Type: parliamentary democracy

Capital City: Baghdad

Chief of State: President Jalal Talabani (since 2005, next election 2014)

Head of government: Prime Minister Nouri Maliki (since 2006)

Independence: October 3, 1932

> *From League of Nations mandate under British administration. On June 28, 2004 the Coalition Provisional Authority transferred sovereignty to the Iraqi Interim Government*

Population: 30,399,572 (July 2011 est.)

Ethnic Groups: Arab 75-80%; Kurdish 15-20%; Turkmen; Assyrian and others 5% (2011)

Religion: 97% Muslim (Shi'a 60-65%, Sunni 32-37%); Christian or other 3% (2011)

Languages: Arabic (official); Kurdish (official in the Kurdish regions); Turkoman (a Turkish dialect); Assyrian; Armenian

Literacy: Total pop. 74.1%: male 84.1%; female 64.2% (2000 est.)

Currency: 1 Iraqi Dinar = 1000 fils or 20 dirhams.

> *(In January 2004, the new Iraqi dinar became Iraq's official currency. Pictures of an ancient Babylonian ruler, a 10th century mathematician and an Islamic compass replace images of Saddam Hussein on the new bills)*

Exports: crude oil 84%, also food and live animals

Proven Oil Reserves: 115 bbl (2010 estimate)

Export partners: U.S. 28%; India 14%, Italy 10%; S. Korea 9% (2009)

Import partners: Turkey 25%, Syria 17%, U.S. 9%, China 6.8% (2009)

GDP per capita: $3,600 (2010) (up from $1,900 per year in 2006)

Unemployment: 15.3% (2009) (down from 25% to 30% in 2005)

Size: 168,709 sq. mi., roughly the size of California (36 mi. of coastline)

Major Cities: Baghdad; Basra; Mosul; Kerbala; Kirkuk

Figures taken from the CIA World Factbook 2011 – Iraq

Iraq in a Nutshell

ANCIENT HISTORY

Iraq's borders roughly correspond to the area considered the "**cradle of civilization**." The ancient region of **Mesopotamia** (meaning "between the rivers" in Greek) developed in the eastern portion of the **Fertile Crescent** between the **Tigris** and **Euphrates** Rivers. It was here that some of the earliest agricultural communities flourished more than 10,000 years ago.

SUMERIANS (2900 B.C. – 2000 B.C.)
The Bronze Age Sumerians, who moved to Mesopotamia 5000 years ago, learned to tame the unpredictable rivers with complex irrigation systems and tilled the lands with the earliest known plows. The sophisticated methods allowed farmers to produce a surplus of food freeing the rest of the population to engage in nonagricultural pursuits (such as specialized skilled labor, trade, religion and state-building)

To facilitate the distribution of the harvests and manage trade and resources, the Sumerians introduced the first form of writing. Commercial transactions were documented
on clay tablets using wedge-shaped letters called **cuneiform**.[1] To keep track of large exchanges, the Sumerians applied mathematical formulae based on a "**sexigesimal**" system (based on numerical 60 as opposed to our base ten which is "decimal"). The modern-day 24-hour clock, which is divided into 60 minutes and 60 seconds, derives directly from this system.

Because of the unpredictable nature of the Tigris and Euphrates rivers and the brutally hot temperatures in summer, the Sumerians had a relatively pessimistic outlook on life. They believed that humans beings lived at the mercy of capricious gods who constantly needed to be appeased to stop them from wreaking havoc.[2] Those who claimed to be able to communicate with the gods (the priests or *ensi*) maintained high positions in society – higher, at least

---

1 The Sumerians wrote with a reed stylus that left a wedge-shaped impression on the wet clay.
2 Sumerians often erected small household shrines with statues of themselves in a perpetual state of supplication so they appeared as if they were praying continuously. Large open eyes (sometimes inlaid with blue lapis lazuli gems imported from the Afghanistan region) were intended to show a state of alertness, even when the worshippers were sleeping. (See image above).

initially, than the local warlords (called the *lugals* or "big men").

To further pacify the gods, each city-state was dedicated to one of the hundreds of gods in the Sumerian pantheon who would be honored in temples built atop massive man-made, pyramid-like, brick[3] structures called **ziggurats**.

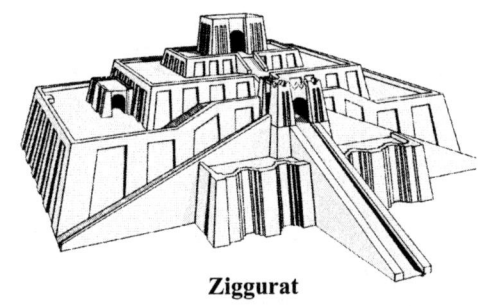
Ziggurat

Eventually the various city-states became more consolidated as the larger communities swallowed up the smaller ones. But the empire was not cohesive enough to withstand the force of a group of Semitic-speaking people from the city of Akkad.

AKKADIANS (2334 B.C. – 2125 B.C.)

The mastermind behind the Akkadian expansion from Elam in Iran to the cedar forests of present-day Lebanon was **Sargon the Great**[4] (r. 2334-2279 B.C.) According to Sargon's own accounts of his life, the Akkadian leader had been saved from death as an infant when his mother, possibly a temple-prostitute, sent him down a river in a basket of rushes sealed with bitumen (a tar-like petroleum product). He was found and raised by **Akki**, a "drawer of water," and worked as a gardener for the **King of Kish** – that is, until Sargon overthrew the king and built his own empire.

One by one, Sargon and his army[5] conquered and subdued neighboring city-states eventually creating the first multi-ethnic empire in the world from the Persian Gulf to the Mediterranean Sea.

SUMERIAN/AKKADIAN PANTHEON
An (Anu) – Sky god
Ki (Antu) – Earth goddess, consort of An
Annunaki – Children of An and Ki
Enlil (Ellil) – God of air, chief deity
Enki (Ea) – God of water
Inanna (Ishtar) – Goddess of love and war

---

3 Since Mesopotamia lacked rocks and wood, the Sumerians learned the art of brickmaking using the regions abundant supply of mud.
4 Sargon's name in Akkadian was "Sharru-kin" or "legitimate king."
5 Sargon created the first known professional standing army in history. His troops, who rode chariots (a Sumerian invention) and wielded copper weapons, were also the first to wear protective helmets..

Iraq in a Nutshell

After unifying the Mesopotamian city-states, standardizing the weights and measures, and promoting the Semitic Akkadian language, the Akkadians let the existing communities have nominal control over their cities. By adopting the Sumerian system of government, economy, law, religion and even their folklore, the Akkadians virtually became Sumerians themselves and spread the culture over their vast empire.

The Akkadians had been so successful in consolidating their power over the region that their language remained the *lingua franca* for centuries in the Middle East and future kings of Mesopotamia proudly addressed themselves as the rulers of "Sumer and Akkad."

But the empire declined in the 22nd century B.C., when the Akkadians, along with neighboring civilizations, fell victim to a global climate change that caused reduced rainfall, drought, salinization and eventually crop failures.[6]

AMORITES OR OLD BABYLONIANS (1900 B.C. – 1600 B.C.)

As the Akkadian empire declined, a nomadic Semitic-speaking people began to migrate from Syria into Mesopotamia – possibly in search of greener pastures during the same change in weather patterns that had devastated the Akkadian region.

After arriving in Mesopotamia, the nomads or **Amorites** (as they were called by the Akkadians after the name of the god they worshipped, **Amurru**), assimilated into Sumero-Akkadian life and soon founded their own cities of Isin, Larsa, Eshnunna and **Babylon**. But the Amorites were not unified until the rise of the 6th king of Babylon, **Hammurabi** (r. 1795-1750 B.C.). About 30 years into his reign, Hammurabi, like Sargon before him, began to conquer neighboring city-states until the region was unified once again from the Persian Gulf to the Syrian border.

Hammurabi's greatest legacy, though, was his law code. Though his wasn't the first written law of the time, the 8-foot tall **Hammurabi stele** (an upright, inscribed stone slab) on which the code was carved, was the largest of its kind to have been found intact.

Among the 282 legal pronouncements were rules determining specific

---

[6] The 22nd c. B.C. climate change (also called the 4.2 kiloyear BP ["before present"] event) may have also caused the decline of the Old Kingdom in Egypt and the gradual collapse of the Harappan civilization in the Indus Valley.

prices, fees and wages to be charged as well as commercial, family and property law. Justice was based on one's status in society (upper class, freeman or slave). Crimes committed by and against members of the same class were punished equally; for instance, "if a man put out the eye of another man, his eye shall be put out."[7] But if the crime was committed against someone from a lower status, the perpetrator would only have to pay a fine. Other penalties were particularly harsh (for example "if a slave says to his master that he is not his master, his ear shall be cut off" and "if a son strikes his father, his hands will be cut off").

HITTITES (1600 B.C. – 1100 B.C.)
The Indo-European Hittites, originating in Anatolia (modern-day Turkey), pioneered the Iron Age by developing furnaces hot enough to melt iron and then combining the metal with carbon to make steel. They used the new technology to produce superior chariots, armor and weapons giving them a great military advantages over neighboring tribes.

By 1595 B.C., the Hittites occupied Babylon from where they conducted raids against Syria and Palestine. The great size of the Hittite empire and their active

---

IRAQ IN THE BIBLE

* The Bible places the location of the **Garden of Eden** (the abode of the first man [Adam] and first woman [Eve]) at the source of four rivers: the Pison, Gihon, Hiddekel (believed to be the Tigris River) and Euphrates

* Traditionally Ur, in present-day Iraq, was considered the birthplace of Judaism and of Islam's patriarch **Abraham**.

* The story of **Noah** and the flood resembles a Sumerian legend about an old man who was granted immortality after surviving 40 days and 40 nights of rain in an ark. The story was recounted in the **Epic of Gilgamesh**, one of the earliest known written stories.

* According to the Bible, the **Tower of Babel** (the biblical name for Babylon) was built by a Mesopotamian tyrant called Nimrod in defiance of God. As punishment, God confused the languages of the population and scattered them. The materials used to build the tower and its intention (to reach the heavens) resembled the construction and aims of Sumerian Ziggurats.

* The story about the infancy of **Sargon of Akkadia** resembles that of the Hebrew prophet and lawgiver Moses. Soon after they were born, both were placed in a basket of rushes sealed with bitumen by their mothers and set afloat down a river. Both were found and raised in royal households.

---

[7] This type of law, called the *lex talionis* or "law of *talion*" (that is, punishment being identical to the offense) can also be found in the Hebrew Bible and the Quran.

Iraq in a Nutshell

trading fostered the spread of Mesopotamian customs and ideas throughout Syria, Palestine, and eventually to Egypt, Greece and the Mediterranean region. The Hittite Empire began to disintegrate into independent city-states by 1180 – units too weak to withstand attacks by the Sea Peoples, a confederacy of seafaring raiders who swept through the Mediterranean, and the Assyrians.

ASSYRIANS (1200 B.C. – 612 B.C.)

The Assyrian kingdom first developed in the 20th century B.C. with the unification of the cities of Arbil, Ashur (named after the Assyrians highest god Assur – from where they get their name) and Nineveh, their capital, near the northern portion of the Tigris River. After a brief period of military expansion in the 14th c. B.C., the Assyrians entered a time of decline or "dark age."

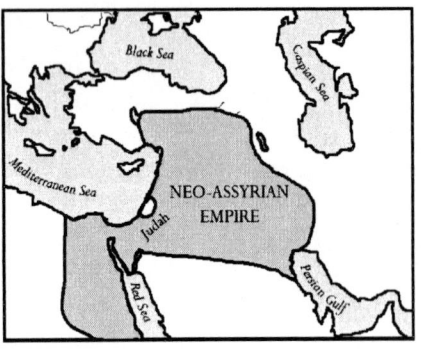

Because of continuous threats from their neighbors during the "dark age," the Assyrians became very militaristic. To defend themselves, they built the largest standing army in the region at that time and employed the most technologically innovative weapons.

Neo-Assyrians

By the 10th c. B.C., the Assyrians' new weaponry and aggressive military training allowed them to take over communities from as far north as Armenia and west to the Nile River in Egypt. In order to prevent revolts in the occupied areas, they forced conquered peoples who refused to worship their gods and accept Assyrian domination to migrate to other areas in the empire, (a tactic used by Saddam Hussein centuries later). After the Assyrians under the rule of **Sargon II**[8] took **Samaria** (the Hebrew's northern kingdom), they forced the tribes of Israelites living in the area to relocate to other parts of the Assyrian empire. In their new land, the displaced Hebrews assimilated and, in Jewish history, became eternally known as the "**Ten Lost Tribes**."

The brutal Assyrians were finally defeated in 612 BC when insurgents

---

[8] The Assyrians considered themselves descendents of the Akkadians hence Sargon II was named after his perceived predecessor, Sargon the Great of Akkadia.

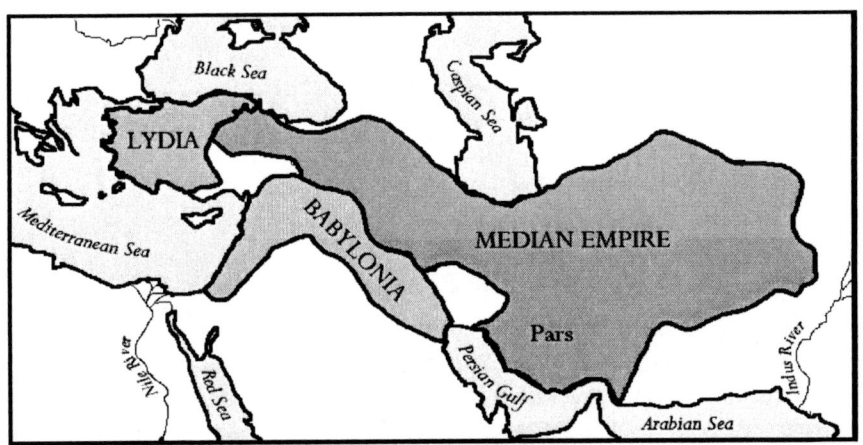

from the city-state of Babylon (the "Neo-Babylonians"), Egyptians, Lydians, and Medes from Iran joined together and burned down the Assyrian capital city of **Nineveh**.

CHALDEANS OR "NEO-BABYLONIANS" (612 B.C.– 539 B.C.)
After the fall of Assyria, the former empire was divided among the victors: Egypt was returned to the Egyptians, the Medes controlled the north and the Babylonians (also known as the Chaldeans) took control of the region between the Tigris and Euphrates Rivers.

Under the greatest of the "New Babylonian" rulers, **King Nebuchadnezzar II** (r. 605-562 B.C.), Babylon was restored to its former splendor. The most famous city in the world was adorned with a new temple, built to honor the Babylonian god **Marduk**,[9] and the famous **Hanging Gardens of Babylon** were constructed with fragrant plants and trees from Iran to please Nebuchadnezzar's homesick Median wife **Amytis**.[10]

Like the Assyrians, the Chaldeans also adopted the practice of deporting uncooperative subjects to other parts of the empire in order to prevent local rebellions. After Nebuchadnezzar II conquered the remaining southern Hebrew kingdom of **Judah** in 587 B.C. and destroyed their temple,

---

[9] Under Nebuchadnezzar II, Marduk the patron deity of Babylon, was elevated above the Sumerian/Akkadian "god of the sky," **An (Anu)**, and the "lord of wind" and ruler of the gods **Enlil** (who was believed to have been responsible for sending a devastating flood that killed all human beings except the mortal Utnapishtim and his family who had been forewarned by another god. [see section on "Iraq in the Bible" pg. 5]).

[10] The Median princess Amytis was married to Nebuchadnezzar to seal the alliance between the Medes and Chaldeans. The site of the Hanging Gardens of Babylon was once listed in ancient Greek guidebooks as one of the Seven Wonders of the World.

Iraq in a Nutshell

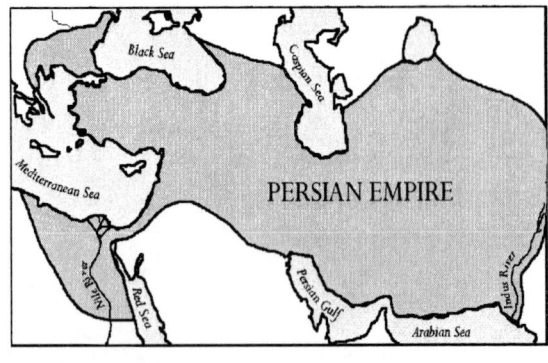

he moved thousands of the most important members of the population (priests, professionals, craftsmen etc.) to Babylon. Unlike the "**Ten Lost Tribes**," though, the Judean Hebrews or "**Jews**" stayed together during their **Babylonian captivity** and continued to observe Jewish practices. While living in exile, the priests (who, without a Temple to perform rituals, had become scribes and sages) decided to record the history of the Israelites – in part to try to understand why God had forsaken them – compiling the information, as well as laws and customs, into the **Torah**.[11] It was also during the period of captivity that synagogues were established as new centers for worship. But the Hebrews never forgot the importance of the Holy Temple in Jerusalem that had been razed by the Babylonian king. Daily the Jews prayed in the direction of their homeland and promised that they would one day return and rebuild the holy site.

When the Babylonian Empire fell to the Persians a few decades later, Persian King **Cyrus the Great** permitted the Hebrews to return to Jerusalem and rebuild their temple.

PERSIAN EMPIRE (539 B.C. – 331 B.C.)

While the Medes were preoccupied with their battle against the Assyrians, a local king from the Pars region of the Median Empire called **Cyrus** was forming a coalition of tribes that soon grew powerful enough to overthrow their Median overlords. After defeating the Medes in 550 B.C., Cyrus (the Great) and the soldiers of his new Persian **Achaemenid** dynasty made their way west across northern Mesopotamia to Asia Minor (present-day Turkey) incorporating the rich kingdom of Lydia[12] into the Empire. The defeat of Lydia and the rebellions that followed eventually led to years of Greco-Persian wars.

---

11 The Torah, also called the Pentateuch, refers to the first five books in the Judeo-Christian Bible (Genesis, Exodus, Leviticus, Numbers, Deuteronomy).

12 The Lydians (who were the first people in history to produce gold and silver coins) were ruled by King Croesus, the richest man in the world at that time. (The expression " to be as rich as Croesus" indicating great wealth, refers to the Lydian king.)

By the time **Darius I**, took power in 522 B.C., the Persian Empire extended from India in the east to Macedonia in the northwest and Egypt in the southwest.[13] The vast Persian Empire spanned three continents and incorporated 20% of the world's population from more than two dozen nations.[14] Not surprisingly, every Achaemenid monarch (or *shah-an-shah* **[king of kings]**) ended up devoting much time and expense to subdue rebellions – including uprisings in the restive region of Lydia.

As long as the Lydians could count on their Greek neighbors for help, the Persians knew the disturbances would never fully be quelled. Although the Greek city-states were less organized and less numerous as the powerful Achaemenid army (which included the famous ten thousand-strong elite force called the Immortals[15]) the Persians' first attempt to take Greece was thwarted in 490 B.C. by the Athenians in the momentous **Battle of Marathon.** A decade later, in 479 B.C. they were again, finally, defeated by an alliance of Greek city-states at the **Battle of Plataea**. The Persians were forced to retreat to Anatolia but remained a formidable neighbor until the Achaemenid empire was conquered a century and a half later by the armies of **Alexander the Great.**

ALEXANDER THE GREAT (330 B.C. – 323 B.C.)
Once the Persians were kept at bay, the Greek city-states began to quarrel among themselves. Years of conflict (e.g. the **Peloponnesian Wars** from 431-404 B.C.), left the city-states weak and vulnerable – too weak, in fact, to defend themselves against the onslaught of Macedonian troops from the northeast under the command of Macedonian **King Philip II.**

In 332 B.C. Philip II was assassinated by a disgruntled former guard and male lover,[16] but his son and successor, **Alexander III**, carried on his

---

13 Cyrus's son Cambyses II defeated Egypt in 525 B.C. but died without an heir. After a power struggle, the Persian throne went to Darius the Great who divided the empire into districts called *"satrapies,"* built the "Royal Road" from Sardis to Susa and even constructed a canal connecting the Red Sea to the Mediterranean Sea among other accomplishments

14 Reliefs carved into the walls of the old Achaemenid palace in the ceremonial capital of Persepolis showed delegates from 23 subject nations in the empire giving tribute to Darius I.

15 Greek historian Herodotus dubbed the elite corps the "Immortals " because every soldier who was killed or wounded was immediately replaced, keeping the number consistent and seemingly "immortal."

16 There has been some suspicion that Philip's assassin may have been supported by Olympia, Philip's former wife and Alexander's mother, who feared that Philip's new wife might bear a son who would take Alexander's place as successor to the Macedonian throne.

Iraq in a Nutshell

father's expansionist ambitions by consolidated Macedonian rule over the Greek city-states and then setting off to conquer Greece's longtime enemy, the Persian Empire.

After a number of swift victories (at the **Battle of Granicus River** [334 B.C.], the **Battle of Issus**, [333 B.C.] and the **Battle of Gaugamela** [331 B.C.]), Alexander and his troops marched into Babylon and then to Persepolis, the ceremonial capital of the Persian Achaemenid Empire. After a drunken celebration, Alexander's troops set the city's palaces ablaze and looted more than 120,000 talents of gold (about $60 billion today). Even after distributing much of the treasure to his generals, Alexander the Great had become the wealthiest man in the world.

A year later (330 B.C.), the Persian Achaemenid emperor, **Darius III**, was killed by the *satrap* (provincial governor) of Bactria, effectively rendering Alexander the de facto ruler of the former Persian Empire. Victorious, Alexander used his newly acquired wealth to establish a number of cities in his new empire – naming most of them after himself.[17]

By the time he was thirty years old, Alexander of Macedonia ruled a territory that stretched from the Adriatic Sea to present-day Pakistan and had lost only one battle – against his own soldiers. Exhausted from years of campaigns away from home and fearful of the powerful Indian armies across the Hyphasis (Beas) River in Punjab, Pakistan, Alexander's troops rebelled against their leader. Alexander was forced to retreat from what would become the farthest eastern border of his empire. Three years later, he died in Babylon – leaving no heir.

SELEUCID EMPIRE (323 B.C. – 170 B.C.)

After Alexander's death in 323 BC, the territory he had conquered was divided among dozens of rival generals, friends and *satraps* (governors) collectively called the "**Diadochi**." After more than twenty years of battle, three of Alexander's generals emerged victorious. **Ptolemy I**, a childhood friend of Alexander, maintained his kingdom in Egypt, **Antigonus** and his successors ruled the Macedonian/Greek territories and **Seleucus I Nicator**, the *satrap* of Babylon, commanded an empire that, at its height, spanned from the Mediterranean Sea to Afghanistan.

---

[17] Many of the newly established cities bore the name Alexandria (for example, Alexandria in Egypt and **Iskandariya** – the Arabic translation for Alexander – south of Baghdad, Iraq where Saddam kept his "super guns" that reached several hundred miles). One city, Alexandria Bucephalous in present-day Pakistan was named after Alexander's beloved horse.

Iraq in a Nutshell

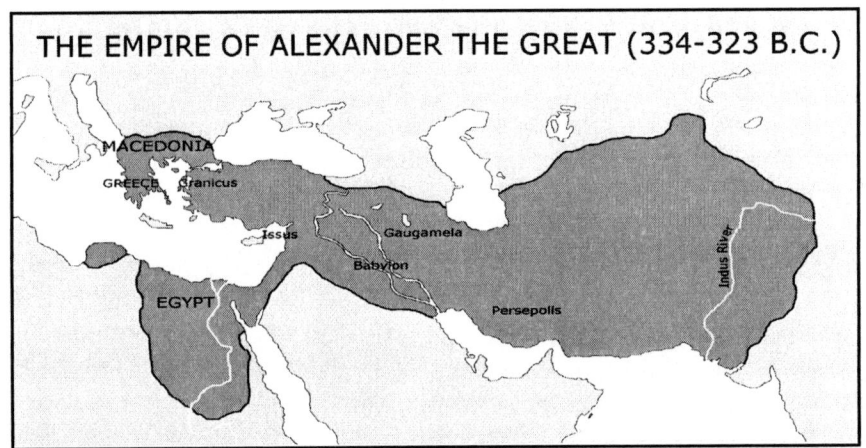

Within his Hellenistic (Greek)[18] empire, Seleucus founded a number of cities including the first capital city of Seleucia on the Tigris River and Antioch,[19] the Seleucid's second capital, in northern Syria which he named after either his father or his son (both named Antiochus).

PARTHIANS (170 B.C. – A.D. 224)

In the middle of the 3rd century B.C., a portion of the eastern Seleucid empire became independent when a tribe of nomads from the Central Asian steppes created their own kingdom of **Parthia**. Under their most successful king, **Mithridates the Great** (171-138 B.C.), the Parthians began expanding east, attacking the kingdom of Bactria,[20] and then, when their eastern border was secure, to the west.

By 144 B.C., the Parthians had reached Babylon and, just a few miles south of Baghdad, established their own winter capital three years later in the new city of **Ctesiphon** across the river from Seleucia.[21] Graced with luxurious palaces and temples, Ctesiphon was coveted by the Romans who captured and then lost the city a half a dozen times between the 2nd

---

18 Although the Seleucids did not force the population to adopt Greek culture, Greek ideas did seep into Mesopotamia – especially among the local educated classes. Both Greek and Aramaic were used as written languages in the government and temples and statues dedicated to Greek gods were erected in cities with large Greek populations.

19 Antioch (now called "Antakya" and located in present-day southern Turkey) would become famous as the city where the disciples of Jesus Christ were first called "Christians."

20 Bactria is the ancient name for a region that included parts of Afghanistan, Uzbekistan and Tajikistan.

21 When the Arabs came to Mesopotamia they joined Seleucia and Ctesiphon by a bridge and called them jointly Mada'en ("the cities").

and 4th centuries A.D..

SASSANIDS (A.D. 224 – A.D. 637)

The Parthian empire was vast but decentralized. Several languages were spoken and different currencies were used in what became a conglomerate of kingdoms and provinces ruled by more than 18 vassal kings.

One of those kings, **Ardashir I**, from the Persian city of Istakhr near Persepolis, rebelled against his Parthian overlords and established his own powerful **Sassanid** empire. Ruling from their adopted capital of Ctesiphon, the Sassanid kings established Zoroastrianism as the state religion and formed a military that was strong enough to keep the hostile Romans at bay.

But while the Eastern Roman Byzantines and Persian Sassanids battled over Mesopotamia's wealthy cities, a more powerful force was growing in a comparatively peaceful region to the southwest, the Muslims of Arabia.

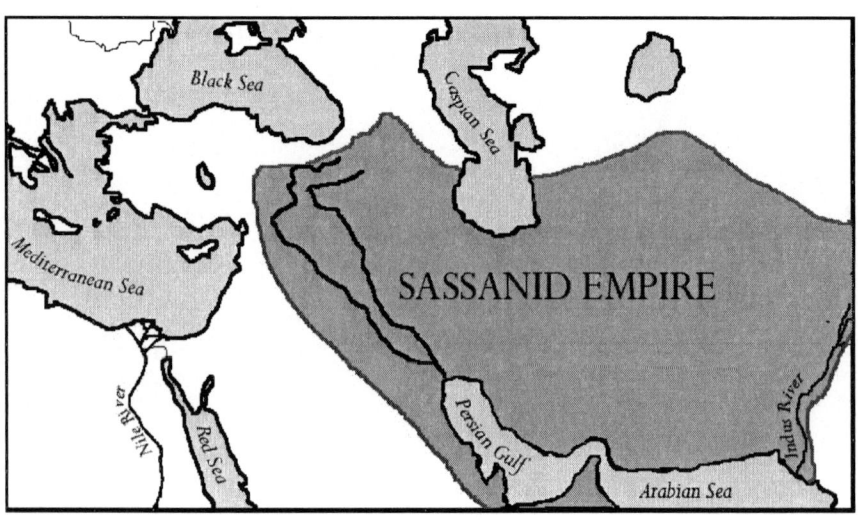

INTRODUCTION OF ISLAM

The course of history dramatically changed when a group of people from the Arabian Peninsula recognized **Muhammad**, born in A.D. 570 in Mecca (in modern-day Saudi Arabia), as the final Prophet of God. The Prophet Muhammad united the formerly polytheistic tribes of Arabia under the monotheistic banner of Islam and spread God's (Allah's) messages, chronicled in the **Quran**, throughout the region. After his death in 632, his first successor or *Caliph,* **Abu Bakr** (r. 632-634) expanded Islam's influence and the Arabic language beyond Arabia's borders to Palestine, Syria and Egypt.

Under Abu Bakr's successor, the second of the four "**Rightly Guided Caliphs,**"[22] **Umar ibn al Khattab** (r. 634-644), the Muslims overtook the Persian **Sassanid Empire** and conquered much of the eastern portion of the **Byzantine (Eastern Roman) Empire** (Byzantium).

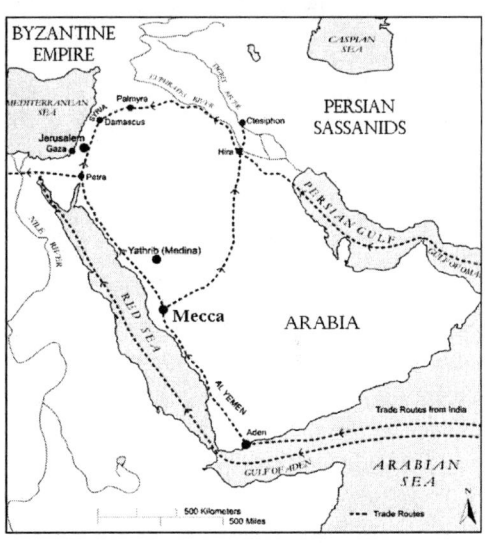

The new religion reached Mesopotamia in A.D. 634 when an army of Arab Muslims under the leadership of General **Khalid ibn al Walid** (nicknamed the "Sword of Islam") defeated the militarily superior Sassanids in the "**Battle of the Chains**" (so-named because the Persian troops were reportedly chained together to prevent them from fleeing).

During another victorious battle in A.D. 636, the Arabs, though outnumbered by their foes, again defeated the Persian Sassanids. This time the Persians were forced to embrace Islam or pay a tribute tax (*jizya*) to their Muslim overlords. The legacy of this "**Battle of Qadisiyyah**" was resurrected centuries later by **Saddam Hussein** who equated his own numerically inferior Iraqi Arab troops fighting the larger Persian (Iranian) army

---
[22] The first four leaders of the *Umma* (the Muslim community) were considered "rightly guided" since they were all either elected or chosen by their predecessors.

Iraq in a Nutshell

during the 1980-1988 Iran-Iraq War with the early Muslims victory over the better equipped Persian Sassanids.

The ultimate collapse of the Sassanid Empire in A.D. 638 marked the beginning of Arab dominance in the region, the establishment of Islam as the official religion and the dawn of the golden age of Muslim culture.

SHI'AS (see Shi'ites pg. 74)

When Islam's Prophet Muhammad died in 632, he had not formally designated a successor. A small group of Muslims, calling themselves the *Shi'at Ali*, the "Party of Ali," or **Shi'as** (Shi'ites) for short, believed that Muhammad's cousin and son-in-law, **Ali ibn Abu Talib,** a blood relative, should have succeeded him as Islam's leader despite his young age. Their wishes were ignored by the council of nobles who instead elected Muhammad's companion, Abu Bakr, as the first caliph (successor). More than 20 years later, Ali was appointed Islam's fourth caliph but his term was short-lived. After Ali was assassinated, his son, **Hassan,** briefly took the post but his reign was contested by the governor of Damascus, Syria, **Muawiya.**

UMAYYAD DYNASTY

After Ali's assassination in 661, Muawiya, the governor of Syria, became caliph introducing the first hereditary dynasty of the Muslim Caliphate. Muawiya's ascendancy as Islam's caliph in 661 and the appointment of Muawiya's son, **Yazid**, as his successor infuriated the Shi'as who marched against the caliphate in rebellion. In October 680, the 10th day (***ashura***) of the Muslim month of **Muharram**, the small band of Shi'as led by Muhammad's grandson, Ali's son **Husayn** (who traveled from Mecca to the Shi'a stronghold in **Kufa**), were met in the city of **Kerbala** by tens of thousands of Yazid's soldiers. According to the Shi'a narrative, Husayn and more than 70 men in his group were killed by Yazid's soldiers and the rest, including women and

14

children, were made captives. Yazid remained caliph of the Umayyad Dynasty for the next three years.

From their capital in **Damascus**, Syria, the **Umayyads** (named after Muawiya's great-grandfather, Umayya ibn Abd Shams) expanded the Islamic empire west to Morocco and east to the present-day border of India. But the Umayyad caliphs were condemned for their secularism, oppressive rule and discrimination against non-Arab Muslims.

Discontent reached a peak in 750 when a group of Muslim rebels descended from Prophet Muhammad's uncle **Abbas**, rose to power. The **Abbasids** killed almost all the members of the Umayyad ruling family and moved the center of activity from Syria to **Mesopotamia** (in part to bring the seat of power closer to the empire's Persian Muslim constituents).

ABBASID DYNASTY
In 762, **Abd al Abbas,** the first caliph of the Abbasid Dynasty, founded the city of **Baghdad** near ancient Babylon and made it the political seat of the caliphate. By the 10th century, the city had become the intellectual center of the world, second in size only to **Constantinople** (present-day Istanbul, Turkey). The new city attracted philosophers, scholars, scientists, and a bevy of traders traveling along the **Silk Route** that linked Asia to the Mediterranean.

At the height of its splendor, Baghdad had a university, many palaces, a library and a teaching hospital. Some of the greatest minds of the time called Baghdad home including **Muhammad ibn Musa Khawarizmi** (680-750) who is credited with inventing Algebra and first applying the Hindu numeric system (today called **Arabic numerals**) to modern mathematics.[23]

Baghdad's glory faded near the end of the 10th century when the center of Muslim intellectual life shifted again away from Baghdad to the capital of the equally powerful **Fatimid dynasty** in the newly established city of **Cairo**, Egypt. The rivalry for dominance over the Islamic world between Baghdad and Cairo raged on from that point on.

Decline of the Abbasid Dynasty
Though still intact, central political control of the Abbasid Caliphate dis-

---
23 Many of the stories collected in the Arabic work, **One Thousand and One Nights**, about a queen (Scheherazade) who tried to delay her death by keeping her husband engaged in the many tales she told (among them the story of Ali Baba and the Forty Thieves and the stories about Sinbad the Sailor) were set in Baghdad in this period.

integrated as local governors asserted their independence and successor Muslim states split off from the empire. Weakened, the Abbasids were unable to prevent the capture of Baghdad by the Persian **Buyids** in 945 or the advance of the **Seljuk Turks** in 1055. Both the Buyids and the Turks continued to recognize the religious and ceremonial authority of the Abbasid caliph even after they had taken over administrative control.

SELJUK (SELJUQ) TURKS

The Seljuk Turks, one of the clans of the Turkish Oghuz tribal confederacy, began pouring into Persia[24] from their homeland in Central Asia in 1037. Once they had claimed their territory, the recent converts to Sunni Islam, who had little experience with government, adopted the Persian system of statecraft and revived the Persian culture and language (letting Arabian influence wane).[25]

By 1055, the Seljuk Turk sultan **Tugrul** had expanded the empire northwest to Baghdad and then into Armenia. Sixteen years later (in 1071), the Seljuk forces penetrated the Byzantine territory of Anatolia by way of **Manzikert** where the armies of **Alp Aslan** (Tugrul's successor and great grandson of Seljuk, the clan's namesake) captured the Byzantine emperor, **Romanos IV Diogenes**.

Romanos was released a week later in exchange for 10 million gold pieces, the release of Muslim prisoners and the city of Manzikert, but the Byzantine empire never fully recovered from the defeat and the ensuing civil war. The weakened state of the Byzantine Empire and the Turkish-Muslim control of Jerusalem prompted the Roman Pope **Urban II** to call for a **Crusade** to recover the "holy land" (the Levant) from the Muslim "infidels."

MONGOLS

In the 13th century, Mesopotamia fell victim to another, more brutal invader from the east, the **Ilkhanate Mongol** hordes of **Hulagu Khan** (1217-1265), grandson of the infamous Great Khan, **Temujin** (better known as **Genghis Khan**). Unlike the more peaceful Turks (who escaped the onslaught by moving into their western domain in Anatolia), the Mongols wreaked havoc in Mesopotamia: massacring the citizens, flattening cities, plundering the country's riches, destroying the irrigation

---

24 Persia by that time had become weak from internal dissent and economic problems.

25 The Persian mathematician, astronomer and poet Omar Khayyam wrote his great works during this time.

canals and leaving the countryside in ruins.[26]

In the course of the 1258 Mongolian **Siege of Baghdad**, several hundreds of thousands of the city's inhabitants were killed, palaces, hospitals and the Grand Library of Baghdad were burned to the ground and the caliph was reportedly wrapped in a carpet and trampled to death by Mongol horses.[27] The **Ilkhanate** (the branch of the Mongolian empire in Iran, Iraq, Afghanistan, Turkmenistan and the Caucasus) didn't last long (1256-1335) but the damage done by the Mongols obliterated Baghdad's splendor for centuries and brought a decisive end to Islam's Golden Age.

TAMERLANE

The Mesopotamian region was subjected to another brutal conquest in 1401 by the Turkish regent from Transoxiana (modern Uzbekistan), **Timur the Lame** or **Tamerlane** (1336-1405).

By the time of Tamerlane's conquest, Mesopotamia had been suffering a severe economic depression due to the destruction of its farming capabilities and the loss of its status as a commercial center. The urban way of life in the region had also given way to the revival of a tribal based system of regional rulers (a system that continued until modern times[28]) making Mesopotamia even more vulnerable to attack.

As Tamerlane's empire disintegrated in the 16th century the area became a battleground for the Turkish Ottomans and Persians, as well as the frontline for conflict between Sunni and Shi'a Muslims.

SAFAVID PERSIANS (Shi'ite) (1501-1683)

The Safavids arose from a Turkish Islamic Sufi (Muslim mystic) order in reaction to perceived corruption of Islam by the Mongols. In the mid 15th century, the Safavids adopted the Shi'a branch of Islam and were eager to advance their religion by military means. Of particular interest to the Safa-

---

26 The damage done to Iraq's canals and irrigation projects – and the murder of inhabitants who would might have otherwise repaired the systems – may have been one cause of Iraq's permanent desertification and salinization. Deforestation and the draining of Iraq's marshes between the 1950s and the 1990s further degraded the land. Today only about 13% of Iraq's land is arable.

27 The Mongols believed that the gods would be offended if royal blood touched the earth.

28 Saddam Hussein regularly filled governmental and military posts with members of his own Tikriti tribe.

Iraq in a Nutshell

vids were the Shi'a holy cities of **Kerbala** (where Ali's son, Husayn, was killed by Yazid's troops) and **Najaf** (the location of Ali's tomb).

From their base in **Ardabil** in northwest Iran, the Safavids conquered Azerbaijan, Armenia and the rest of Iran forcing the primarily Sunni population to convert to Shi'a Islam (89% of Iranians today are Shi'a Muslims as a result). In 1507, the Safavids successfully conquered Najaf and Kerbala and in 1508 they took Baghdad and the rest of Iraq from the Aq Qoyunlu (the Sunni Muslim "White Sheep Turkomans" who ruled northern Iraq from 1378 to 1508).

For the next two centuries, the Safavids contended with the rival Sunni-Muslim empire to the west, the **Ottoman Turks,** who jostled for control over the region between the Tigris and Euphrates rivers.

OTTOMAN TURKS (Sunni) (1301-1918)

The Ottoman Empire was founded by Osman I (the source of the name "Ottoman") in 1299 from the ruins of the Seljuk Turkish Sultanate in Anatolia.[29] At its height, the Ottoman Empire had expanded beyond Osman's homeland in western Anatolia (present-day Turkey) to Hungary, the Caspian Sea, the Persian Gulf, across northern Africa and south to Somalia.

In 1453, the Ottoman Turks under the command of Sultan Mehmed II captured **Constantinople**, the last stronghold of the Eastern Roman Byzantine Empire, and made it their capital. The conquest was a watershed moment for both Christians and Muslims. It signaled the end of the Roman Empire and the beginning of the Renaissance in Europe. For the Muslims, it symbolized Islam's victory over Christendom and Ottoman legitimacy as guardians of the Muslim faith. To reinforce the victory, moments after the conquest of Constantinople, Mehmed II ceremoniously converted the famous Hagia Sophia cathedral[30] into a mosque and rechristened the city "Istanbul."

During the rule of the longest reigning and most prominent monarch, **Suleiman the Magnificent** [r. 1520-1566]), the empire stretched from the border of Vienna (in present-day Austria) in Europe, North Africa as far

---

29 The Seljuk Turks who had fled west to Anatolia to escape the onslaught of the Mongols had established the smaller **Sultanate of Rum** (from the Arabic word for the Roman Empire). By the beginning of the 14th century, the sultanate had disintegrated into a number of small principalities or *beyliks*, among them, the *beylik* of Osman.

30 The architecture of the basilica, including its domed roof, became a model for future Islamic mosques.

Iraq in a Nutshell

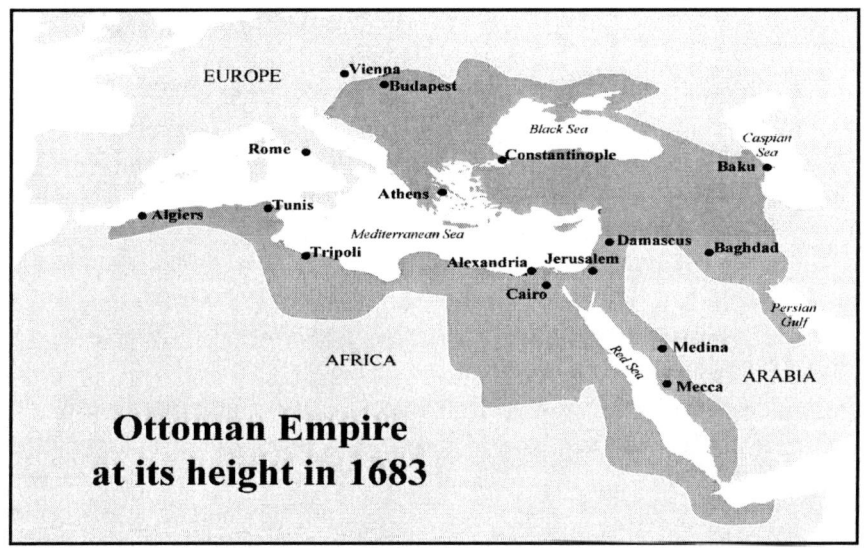

Ottoman Empire at its height in 1683

west as Algeria, south beyond Mecca in Arabia and Sudan in Africa and east to the Persian Gulf. Suleiman's successor, **Selim the Sot** (Selim II), extended Ottoman control further south to Yemen on the Arabian Peninsula and Somalia in eastern Africa and east to the Caspian Sea.

In order to manage the vast territory, the Ottomans divided the empire into *vilayets* or "administrative districts" overseen by governors appointed by the **Sublime Porte** (the Ottoman court of the sultans). The area that would eventually become Iraq comprised of three vilayets: **Mosul** in the north, where most of the Kurds lived; **Baghdad** in the middle; and the primarily Shi'ite *vilayet* of **Basra** in the south.[31]

From the 16th to the 17th centuries, control over modern-day Iraq shifted back and forth between the Persian Safavids and the Turkish Ottomans (with brief stints under the Mamelukes), while none of the victors undertook measures to develop the area. Despite some efforts by the reform-minded governor of Baghdad, **Midhat Pasha,** in 1869, and some sultans after him, to repair and modernize the *vilayets* of Basra, Baghdad and Mosul,[32] the cities of Mesopotamia languished, leaving Iraq the most backward and underdeveloped region in the Ottoman Empire.

---

[31] Saddam Hussein and other Iraqis later claimed that Kuwait, whose borders were within the Ottoman vilayet of Basra when the empire collapsed, was technically part of Iraq. The Kuwaitis countered that the country's independence from the Ottoman Empire long preceded that of Iraq's independence.

[32] The Turks, who considered themselves the "shepherds" to Iraq's "sheep" worked to transform the nomadic tribal society of Iraq back into a settled, agricultural one.

Iraq in a Nutshell

EUROPEAN INTERFERENCE

In 1908, a new ruling clique, the **Young Turks,** took power in Istanbul. The Young Turks endeavored to unify the Ottoman Empire along secular lines and to govern according to Western models. This nationalist group also tried to homogenize the empire by imposing Turkish customs, language and policies on the ethnically and linguistically diverse Ottoman population. The "turkification" movement alienated and angered many of the empire's non-Turkish members, including the Arab Iraqis, who, backed by the British, eventually revolted in protest.

Despite Iraq's backwardness and poverty, the British saw the region as a useful link to its important colony in India. By setting up a postal service that connected east and west via the Euphrates River and land routes traversed on camels, communication between London and the British in India was cut from months (if rounding the tip of Africa) to weeks. To facilitate passage along the routes, Britain established consulates in Basra and Baghdad.

In the 1890s, the Germans, too, made plans to build a railroad that would connect Berlin to resource-rich Baghdad and a proposed German port to be built at the Persian Gulf. Since Africa and Asia had long since been claimed by other colonial powers, the Germans turned to 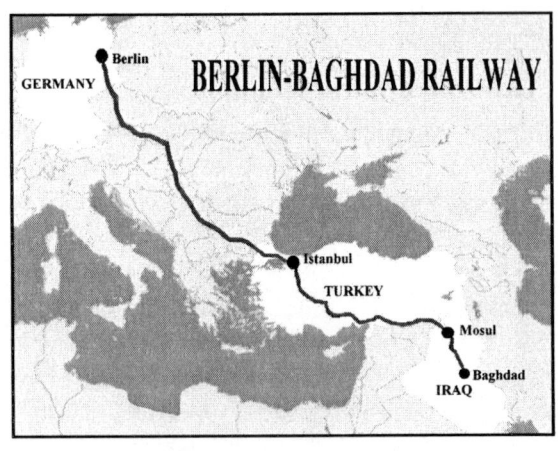 the debt-ridden Ottoman Empire as an ally and outlet for manufactured goods. The area of Mesopotamia (in the Ottoman Empire's eastern *vilayets*) was particularly valuable because it was believed that the lands contained substantial reservoirs of petroleum.

The access to oil increasingly became a significant strategic issue in the years preceding World War I. In 1911, by the suggestion of then Lord of the Admiralty **Winston Churchill**, the British navy converted the energy source powering their ships from burning coal (which England had in

Iraq in a Nutshell

abundance) to burning oil. Since Britain had no known oil of its own, the nation needed to secure a reliable source of the new fuel.

Great Britain had its source after 1908 when oil was discovered in the Khuzestan region of Persia (near the Iraq border in present-day Iran). By 1914, the British government secured direct control of the Persian oil industry but the German presence just west of the valuable oil fields was now seen as a potential threat.

Expecting to secure more potential oil (and to deprive rival Germany from the resource), the British allied with Russia and France in order to squeeze Germany and their Ottoman friends out of the region.

In May 1916, before the Ottoman Empire had been defeated, the British, Russians and French signed a secret agreement dividing Iraq, present-day Turkey and the Ottoman provinces of the Levant into spheres of influence. According to the **Sykes-Picot Agreement**, France would be allocated the territory of south-eastern Turkey, Syria, Lebanon and northern Iraq. The Russians would get Constantinople and the Armenian *vilayets* and Britain would control present-day Jordan and southern Iraq.

WORLD WAR I

Although the heaviest fighting in World War I would take place in Europe, the Middle Eastern theater played a significant role in the ultimate Triple Entente defeat of the Central Powers.

After a victorious battle against the British forces in Gallipoli, for example, the Ottoman Turks strategically blocked access through the Dardanelles cutting the Russians off from their allies. The loss

World War I	
Triple Entente vs.	**Central Powers**
Britain	Germany
France	Austria-Hungary
United States	Ottoman Empire
Russia (until 1917)	

Iraq in a Nutshell

of this supply route further aggravated the already restive Russian population causing them to turn against their Tsar in rebellion. Discontent among the battle-weary Russians and the Revolution prompted the Russians to pull out of the war permanently in 1917.

Of less importance, in June 1915, British troops sailing in from the Persian Gulf occupied Ottoman territory around Kuwait and Basra in southeastern Mesopotamia – ostensibly to protect the British oil fields in Persia. From their base in southwest Iraq, the mostly Indian British troops advanced up the Tigris River until, after a few setbacks, they captured Baghdad in March 1917.

Along with engaging the Ottoman forces in Mesopotamian, the British kept the Turks distracted by fomenting rebellion in the Ottoman territories in western Arabia. To organize the Arabs, the British employed the flamboyant officer **T.E. Lawrence** (popularly known as **Lawrence of Arabia**) who was aided by **Faisal bin Hussein**, son of **Hussein bin Ali**, the **Sharif of Mecca**.[33]

In return for their efforts, the British, represented by High Commissioner **Sir Henry McMahon**, promised Hussein bin Ali in a series of letters (known as the **McMahon-Hussein Correspondence**) that the United Kingdom would recognize Arab independence in a designated region: *"up to the 37th degree of latitude ... on the east by the borders of Persia up to the Gulf of Basra; on the south by the Indian Ocean; ...on the west by the Red Sea; the Mediterranean Sea up to Mersina."*

Lawrence's ragtag tribal Arabian army didn't win any significant military battles (aside from occupying Aqaba in present-day Jordan) but they successfully keep the Ottomans occupied while the British amassed troops at the Suez Canal in Egypt. While Turkish troops were busy repairing rebel-damaged tracks along the Damascus to Medina **Hejaz Railway** in the east, the British, led by Field Marshal **Edmund Allenby**, were advancing from the west. Finally, in September 1917, Lawrence and his Arabs launched a diversionary attack on a rail junction in Deraa in southwestern Syria, allowing British forces to make their way into Damascus. A month later, the Ottomans signed the **Armistice of Mudros** and dropped out of the war. The vanquished empire was dismantled soon after.

---

33 The "Sharif of Mecca" was the governor of the Hejaz (western Arabia) and traditionally the steward of the Islamic holy cities of Mecca and Medina. From 1908 to 1916 the title was held by Hussein bin Ali Pasha, a descendent of Islam's prophet Muhammad's Hashemite clan. (The Hashims were a clan within the larger Quraish tribe).

Iraq in a Nutshell

POST-WORLD WAR I TREATIES

After the defeat of the Ottomans, what was left of the Empire was divided among the victors. According to the terms of the August 1920 **Treaty of Sevres** hashed out in **San Remo**, Italy, present-day Syria and Lebanon were mandated to France, Palestine and the province of Mesopotamia (Iraq) were mandated to Great Britain, Greece was given territory on the west coast of Anatolia and France, Britain and Italy would each be awarded large spheres of influence in present day Turkey. The Treaty of Sevres also provided for an independent Armenia and an autonomous Kurdistan (see section on the Kurds pg. 63).

The dismantling of Anatolia was more than the Turks could bear. As the allies poured into Turkey to claim their portions of the crumbling Empire, the nationalistic Turks began to resist. Under the guidance of army officer and future Turkish president Mustafa Kemal Atatürk, the resistance turned into a war for independence that ended with the annulment of the Treaty of Sevres in favor of a new treaty.

According to the new 1923 Treaty of Lausanne, both the Kurds and the Armenians lost their autonomous nations and Turkey, within its current boundaries, was declared independent.

BRITISH MANDATE

Two years after the British and Arab forces took Damascus the British, in partial fulfillment of their agreement with the Sharif of Mecca, established the short-lived independent Arab Kingdom of Syria crowning Sharif Hussein's son, **Faisal**, the new nation's king on March 7, 1920. Just a few months into his reign, however, France demanded the implementation of the secret 1916 **Sykes-Picot** agreement and the **Treaty of Sevres** granting France control over Syria and Lebanon and expelled Faisal from Syria.

As consolation, the British decided to install Faisal as the king of the newly created country of Iraq.

According to the Sykes-Picot treaty, Britain was entitled to the territories in southern Mesopotamia (the Sunni-dominated *vilayet* of Baghdad and the primarily Shi'a-Muslim *vilayet* of Basra). When oil was discovered in Kurdish-populated **Mosul** in northern Mesopotamia in 1918, the British renegotiated with the French to include Mosul within their zone of

23

Iraq in a Nutshell

influence.[34] The British united the three religiously and ethnically diverse regions into a single entity creating rivalries that continue to this day.

Understandably, the Arabs living in Mesopotamia deeply resented the imposition of yet another foreign power and violently rose up against European rule. The insurrection began with the murder of a British officer in 1919 and escalated in 1920 when the mandate was finalized at the San Remo Conference. More than a thousand British troops were killed by the Iraqi embittered nationalists.

In order to quell the disturbances, the British reconsidered their mandate and decided to back a seemingly more legitimate ruler, the recently deposed son of the Sharif of Mecca and direct descendent of the Prophet Muhammad's Hashim clan (the Hashemites), **Faisal bin Ali**.

Along with his Islamic credentials, Faisal had also fought alongside T.E. Lawrence during WWI and was sympathetic to the British. The fact that Faisal was a Sunni Muslim from Arabia rather than an Iraqi Shi'ite, strained his relationship with Iraqi natives but guaranteed that he would never feel secure enough to alienate himself by defying the British.[35] The British also reasoned that a Sunni-led regime (despite the fact that the country had a Shi'ite majority) would be more acceptable to Iraq's primarily Sunni neighbors. Sunni Muslims continued to dominate the government of Iraq until the war of 2003.

In order to strengthen King Faisal's questionable legitimacy as an Iraqi leader, a carefully calculated plebiscite (election) was held by the British in 1921. After all viable competition was eliminated, Faisal appeared to have won a 96% endorsement by the Iraqis. With superficial political approval, the puppet Hashemite king ruled the country under British authority until agitation by Iraqi nationalists, tribal leaders and even the King himself brought about a series of measures granting the regime greater and greater autonomy. In 1932, after years of lobbying, the British mandate finally came to an end and the country of Iraq was admitted into the **League of Nations** as an independent nation.

Faisal died a year later and was succeeded by his son **Ghazi**. Despite

---

[34] In return for ceding Mosul, the French were offered a quarter interest in what would become known as the Iraq Petroleum Company (IPC).

[35] The British frequently applied the divide-and-rule strategy to prevent coordinated uprisings in their empires.

Iraq in a Nutshell

Iraq's continued economic dependence on Great Britain, Ghazi cast his allegiance in a different direction from his father's. In 1936, Ghazi signed a non-aggression treaty with Saudi Arabia and formed an alliance with other Arab nations. His pan-Arab interests and anti-British sentiments made him popular with many Iraqis, but may have led to his mysterious death in 1939.

In 1939, Ghazi's son and successor, **Faisal II**,[36] was only 3 years old when his father died. Until he came of age, the new monarchy was governed by a regent, **Amir abd al Ilah**, and an Iraqi politician **Nouri as-Said,** both staunchly pro-British.

Said and Ilah's pro-western stances were increasingly at odds with the rest of the Arab world, especially after events such as Egyptian president **Gamal Abdel Nasser's** successful nationalization of the **Suez Canal** in Egypt (1956) and in light of growing bitterness over the high-handed treatment of the Palestinians by the British. After almost three decades of British-backed Hashemite rule in Iraq, the monarchy was finally toppled and the country experienced its first taste of republican government.

COUP D'ETAT

Because the regime under Said and Ilah (and, by 1958, the now-grown Faisal II), didn't tolerate political dissent, opposition groups were forced to operate underground. It was one of these groups, the **"Free Officers"** led by **Brigadier Abdel Karim Kassim (Qasim)**, that staged the decisive coup d'état against the monarchy in 1958. The "Free Officers" killed the entire royal family including the king's uncle and regent Ilah, the prime minister Nuri Said (who was caught trying to escape by dressing as a woman) and their supporters. Five years later (1963), Kassim's government was toppled by a coup that some say was supported by the American **Central Intelligence Agency** (CIA) who regarded the shift of power as a "pro-Western re-orientation in the Middle East."

BAATH (BA'ATH) PARTY

The **Baath** (meaning "resurgence" or "rebirth" in Arabic) movement began as a secular political movement in Syria in the 1930s with the intention of reawakening the common culture of the Arab world in opposi-

---
[36] Faisal II's cousin, Sharif ali bin Hussein, has campaigned for the return of the monarchy in Iraq with himself as king. He currently heads the Iraqi Constitutional Monarchy (ICM) movement. His claim is contested by Prince Raad bin Zeid, grandson of Sharif Hussein and son of Prince Zeid, successor to Faisal II after his assassination in 1958.

Iraq in a Nutshell

tion to western influences. It was formally founded in 1947 as the Arab Baath Socialist Party and achieved political power in Syria soon after. By 1963, the Baath Party was the only party in Syria and, in fulfillment of its socialist agenda, it nationalized the country.

Baath Party Flag

The Syrian-based Baath party had chapters all over the Arab world and campaigned for the equitable distribution of oil wealth (which was concentrated in the hands of a few, mostly foreign capitalists) as well as state ownership of natural resources. It also called for the destruction of the artificial boundaries created by the British and French from the carved-up remains of the Ottoman Empire. They hoped, eventually, to incorporate all the Arab chapters of the party under a single leader.

The Iraqi chapter of the Baath party was founded in the early 1950s under the same banner of **Unity, Freedom and Socialism** as its Syrian parent. Unlike the Syrian branch, though, the Iraqi Baathists remained a small fringe group of intellectuals for most of the 1950s.

The Baathists first asserted their authority in 1959 by attempting (but failing) to assassinate President **Abdel Karim Kassim** because of his perceived close relationship to the Baathists' enemies, the Soviet-backed communists. At the time, official biographers of Iraq's future president, **Saddam Hussein**, himself a Baathist, celebrated Hussein's role in the attempted coup. Other historians, however, claim that Hussein himself was partly responsible for the coup's failure by prematurely opening fire.

In 1963, the Baathists finally succeeded in removing and killing Kassim but they could not muster up enough political muscle to hold on to power. In their place, a larger and more moderate group led by **General Abdul Salam Arif** took control.

Within five years, the Baathists had recruited enough new members and supporters to stage a final and decisive coup against Arif's son, **Salam Arif**. **Ahmed Hassan Bakr** was installed as the new leader and the date, July 17, 1968, was declared the day of "The Great Revolution that ended Iraq's dictatorial regime." To help guarantee the new regime's survival, the Baathists immediately purged the country of all dissidents.

SADDAM HUSSEIN

Saddam Hussein was born on April 28, 1937 in a tribal village near the city of Tikrit in north-central Iraq. His household, like those of other impoverished families living in the village, had no running water and no electricity. The family was so poor that Hussein was reportedly sent to steal chickens and eggs to keep the family fed.

Saddam's father either died soon after Saddam was born (the official government story) or deserted his mother – a scandalous act in Iraq – leaving Saddam fatherless and the target of bullying by other children. He was raised by an abusive stepfather whose family had an even lower social status in the village than his mother and biological father.

Saddam Hussein was born into a local clan, his clan being the **Khattab** clan from the **Bu Nasir** tribe in the **Tikriti** tribal federation. Like other Iraqis, Saddam felt a strong loyalty to his kinsmen and appointed members of his tribe to high government posts when he rose to power later in life.

At age 10, Hussein was sent to Baghdad to live with his uncle **Adnan Khairallah Tulfah**, a devout Sunni Muslim with xenophobic views, particularly against the British and their puppet-monarchy that ruled Iraq at the time. Khairallah, an avid Nazi-sympathizer who once wrote a pamphlet titled "Three Whom God Should Not Have Created: Persians, Jews and Flies," was a hero and mentor to Saddam. Saddam became Khairallah's protégée and was proudly introduced to members of the Sunni elite. It was during his stay with his uncle that Hussein first received an education, though his grades weren't good enough for entrance into Baghdad's prestigious Military Academy (an omission that later fueled his military ambitions).

In keeping with the rural Iraqi custom of maintaining the bonds of kinship and tribal loyalty through intermarriage, Saddam eventually married his favorite uncle's daughter (and his first cousin), **Sajida Khari**, with whom he had two sons (**Uday** and **Qusay**) and three daughters.

Hussein began working for the **Baath Party** in 1956 partly as the party's hit-man. In October, 1959, he participated in the faction's first attempted assassination of **General Kassim**, the prime minister installed

Iraq in a Nutshell

in Iraq after the fall of the Hashemite royal family. Some sources claim that it was Hussein's blunders during the plot that caused it to fail. State biographers, however, lauded Hussein for his heroic role in the incident. After the botched assassination attempt, Hussein and his fellow plotters escaped to Syria and Egypt, where Hussein lived at the time of the Baath Party's second successful (but short-lived) coup against Kassim in 1963.

When the Baathists regained power permanently five years later, supreme authority was passed to **Ahmed Hassan Bakr**, the chairman of the **Revolutionary Command Council** (RCC) (the executive and legislative arm of the Baath Party) who then became president and commander-in-chief of the armed forces. Saddam Hussein became the Deputy Chairman of the RCC in charge of internal security, a position he used to his great advantage. For the next few years, Hussein ran the country from the sidelines using his position in Internal Security to rid the country of potential rivals to the Baath party (which was a minority movement in the beginning) and, more significantly, his own enemies.

Careful not to overstep his boundaries, Hussein dutifully carried out the orders of his uncle's friend and fellow Tikriti, President Bakr, while manipulating the system. As second in command, Hussein was responsible for some of Iraq's most important developments. In 1972, for instance he spearheaded the nationalization of Iraq's oil by brokering an agreement with the Soviets. The deal poured a great deal of money into the country's coffers which enabled the government to build schools, bring electricity to remote regions (like Saddam's home town), develop radio

---

TRIBES

Underneath all ethnic and religious distinctions in Iraq lies an intricate web of tribal affiliations. Each regime that has dominated Iraq has attempted to tap into the dynamics of tribal relations in order to maintain influence over the populace.

At the most intimate level, Iraqis are grouped into families (*khams*) sharing a great-great grandfather. Families are grouped into "houses" or *bayts* which are grouped into clans (*fakdhs*) and tribes (*ashira*). Tribes, which can have from 1000 to 100,000 members, are then organized into confederations or *qabilas*. Each grouping is headed by a *shiekh* who has varying degress of authority in the community.

Today about 75% of the population belongs to one of the country's 150 tribes (*ashiras*) which can trace their ancestry to one of nine tribal confederations.

The largest confederations, the Shammar and Jubur, have both Sunni and Shi'ite members.

and TV networks (used to broadcast Baathist propaganda), build railroads and support all types of modernization. Poor families everywhere were given free televisions so that they could regularly watch Saddam Hussein in action on regular newscasts. [37]

Due to his privileged relationship with President Bakr, Hussein was also able to install his friends, family members and clan associates in the highest governmental positions, further reinforcing his authority. By the time Hussein was ready to take his place at the head of Iraq's government, he already had so much influence in the government that Bakr was simply asked to step down.

In a smooth transition on July 17, 1979, Bakr "retired" from public life and "voluntarily" handed the reins to Hussein. Three years later, Bakr was quietly killed after it was rumored that he was staging a comeback.

One of Hussein's first moves as President was to rid the government of any rivals still surviving after purges conducted in the 1970s. In a filmed spectacle a few days after assuming power, Hussein accused and put to death dozens of Baath Party members on charges of conspiracy – initiating a gruesome system of obedience through intimidation, torture and the threat of death. Hussein, his family members and loyal cronies controlled the media, the army, police and security services. Trade unions and rival parties were banned and opposition was punishable by death.

---

[37] As President, Saddam Hussein reinforced the "cult of personality" by hiring doubles to appear for the media at various functions, freeing himself to perform state tasks. The ruse also made it appear as if Saddam was omnipresent.

IRAN-IRAQ WAR

In 1979, while Saddam Hussein was climbing to the head of Iraq's government, the fundamental Shi'ite cleric, **Ayatollah Khomeini**, was leading his country, Iran, in an Islamic Revolution.

Khomeini's rise to power was threatening to Iraq in a number of ways. First, the Ayatollah, who had been living in exile in Iraq since 1964, had recently been kicked out (in 1978). Second, Hussein feared that the Shi'ites living in Iraq (60% of the population) would be swept up in Iran's Shi'ite revolution and overthrow the mainly Sunni regime. (In fact, the Ayatollah did call on Iraq's Shi'ites to revolt against the Sunni Baathist regime and in response Saddam exiled thousands of Iraqi Shi'ites to Iran). Third, the growing religious fervor in Iran threatened to ignite religious sentiments in secular Iraq. Fourth, Iraq feared that Khomeini would support Kurdish rebellions in northern Iraq as Iran had done in the past.

In the meantime, Iran's strength had been weakened by a purge of military leaders loyal to the Shah of Iran, **Mohammed Reza Pahlavi**, (Iran's former leader) and the instability of the revolution itself. The turmoil gave Hussein the perfect opportunity to champion the cause of Sunni Islam for the rest of the Sunni Arab world and to win glory as a war hero at home. The battle could also be considered another chapter in the historical Persian-versus-Arab, Shi'ite-versus-Sunni rivalry that began in the 16th century.

The Iraqi regime hoped that by capturing **Khuzestan**, a primarily Arab (not Persian) swath of land in western Iran, the country could get its hands on the area's rich oil reserves and possibly trigger an Arab revolution against the new Iranian Islamic government. (The Arabs did not revolt).

Officially, Iraq said it declared war on Iran in order to recapture the valuable **Shatt al-Arab**[38] waterway, Iraq's main shipping route to the Persian Gulf. According to the **Algiers Agreement** of 1975, the international border between Iran and Iraq was placed down the middle of the canal. Iraq had agreed to this in order to persuade Iran to withdraw support for the Kurds, who had been threatening the stability of the Baath party in the north. In 1979 the Iraqi regime claimed that the arrangement

---

[38] Iranians refer to the waterway as Arvand Rud (Arvand River).

was only temporary and that Iraq had the right to control the entire waterway.

Troops were deployed soon after the Algiers Agreement was unilaterally cancelled by Hussein in September 1980, with the conviction that despite Iran's vast size (three times the size of Iraq) the Iraqi military would quickly defeat the Persians (Iranians) – who were struggling in the midst of political turmoil and only had worn-out weapons with which to defend themselves.

But neither Hussein nor the country's military was prepared to counter such strong Iranian resolve. Persian clerics roused hundreds of thousands of religious zealots (including some children) to fight a holy war (*jihad*) against what they labeled "infidel" aggressors. The poorly trained, unarmed **"Army of 20 Million"** cleared minefields for the safe passage of tanks and charged the Iraqi troops en masse in hopes that they would heroically die as martyrs and ascend directly to heaven. The Iraqi troops, in contrast, did not embrace the same spiritual aspirations. On the contrary, many Iraqi fighters were Shi'ite Muslims themselves who were reluctant to fight their religious brothers.

In Iran, jailed pilots and soldiers once loyal to the overthrown Iranian regime were released from prison to join the war and military leaders began to take the place of religious clerics in leading the Persian troops to victory at all costs. The Iraqi generals, on the other hand, were committed to preventing casualties and were hindered by Hussein's insistence that all military personnel answer directly to him.

After an eight-year war of attrition, with neither side claiming any lasting victories, the war took on a global aspect. Western powers began to take notice during one of the **"Tanker Wars"** – battles in the Persian Gulf targeting oil tankers (and hence threatening oil prices) from around the world.

Although most western powers claimed neutrality in the Iran-Iraq War, the majority stood behind the "lesser of two evils," namely Iraq. By the war's end[39] Iraq's political Sunni dominance and secular leanings were more appealing to its primarily Sunni Arab neighbors and the West. Still reeling over the Iranian American **hostage crisis** of 1979, moreover, the United States hoped to contain the fundamental Islamic Revolution brewing in Iran.

Although Iraq's desperate use of chemical weapons against Iran (in violation of the 1925 *Geneva Protocol* on the use of such weapons) would temporarily cause the West to reconsider its allegiances, in 1986 Saddam's empire received enough arms and ammunition to force Iran to negotiate. With the acceptance of **UN Security Resolution 598**, both sides returned to their prewar boundaries. The war was over, albeit with no territorial gains, a million people dead or wounded and the economic structure of both countries in ruins.

---

[39] In 1985, the U.S. provided arms to Iran via Israel to help counter earlier Iraqi successes. The Americans involved in the transaction hoped the Iranians would put pressure on terrorist groups with Iranian ties to free American hostages held in Lebanon. The money from the sale of the arms, moreover, would be used to illegally fund Nicaraguan rebels (the "Contras") opposing Nicaragua's socialist Sandinista National Liberation Front (FSLN). The infamous scandal became known as the Iran-Contra Affair.

Iraq in a Nutshell

GULF WAR

Although Iraq's million-strong army was the largest and most powerful in the Arab world by the end of the 8-year war with Iran, the rest of the country was in shambles. Oil production precipitously dropped during the Iran-Iraq war and many of the country's oil wells were damaged. Reconstruction costs were astronomical. War debts had reached $80 billion and there were no jobs for returning veterans. Although Saddam Hussein tried to claim an Iraqi victory after the costly conflict, the nation was aware that his regime was responsible for a war that cost them hundreds of thousands of casualties with little to show for it. To make matters worse, the profits from oil (Iraq's primary export) had plummeted in the international market due to flooding by other oil producing countries (primarily Russia).

In an attempt to ease all these problems in one fell swoop, Hussein turned his attention to **Kuwait**, a country that was a fraction of the size of Iraq's former foe, Iran, in terms of population and land mass, with an enviable coastline and rich oil reserves.

By targeting Kuwait and demanding that the country forgive Iraq's debt of $13 billion, Iraq hoped to intimidate other lender nations into forgiving the loans they had extended to Iraq during the war with Iran. Hussein also hoped that by attacking the oil-rich nation and curbing its oil producing capabilities, world oil prices would rise and Iraq could take hold of Kuwait's portion of the lucrative **Rumaila Oil Fields** for itself. (Iraq and Kuwait shared ownership of Rumaila, one of the largest proven oil deposits in the world).

IRAQ'S HISTORICAL CLAIM ON KUWAIT
Since the time of the country's creation after World War I from remnants of the Ottoman Empire, Iraqis have claimed Kuwait as their own territory.

Iraq in a Nutshell

As part of the Basra *vilayet*, (one of three administrative areas that made up Iraq after the collapse of the Ottoman Empire), Iraqis believed Kuwait was intended to be included within Iraqi borders. The Kuwaiti issue had been popular in Iraq since British Mandate days and Saddam hoped that by invoking the historical claim, he could repair his political image. The Kuwaitis maintained that they were independent from the Ottomans long before Iraq's creation.

IMPLIED CONSENT IN THE WEST

Saddam expected that the international community, which had supported him against **Ayatollah Khomeini's** fundamental Iranian Shi'ite Muslims, would be sympathetic to Iraq's plight and turn a blind eye to his aggression against the small Gulf state.

In Hussein's mind, the United States (the most formidable superpower left after the fall of the Soviet Empire) had tacitly consented to the attack of Kuwait through U.S. Ambassador to Iraq, **April Glaspie**. In a meeting between the Ambassador and Hussein on July 25, 1990, Glaspie assured Saddam that the U.S. wanted to improve relations with Iraq and had "no opinion on Arab-Arab conflicts such as [Iraq's] dispute with Kuwait."

A few days later, Iraq declared war on Kuwait (which it labeled Iraq's 19th district) on the grounds that Kuwait was deliberately driving down the price of oil by producing too much – an act that Hussein said amounted to "economic warfare" against Iraq – and illegally pumping oil from Iraq's half of the Rumaila oil field. Iraq also claimed that its forces had been "invited" to Kuwait by a rebellious faction that wanted Iraq's help in toppling Kuwait's monarchy.

ATTACK ON KUWAIT

After eight years of war with Iran – ostensibly fought over access through the **Shatt al-Arab** waterway – Hussein gave up full control of Shatt al-Arab to Iran in exchange for a guarantee that the Persians would not incite a Kurdish rebellion in the north while Iraq pursued Kuwait in the south.

Iraq in a Nutshell

Only seven hours after Iraq invaded Kuwait on August 2, 1990, the country was completely in Iraqi hands. The Kuwaitis were terrorized and the only member of Kuwait's royal family who remained in the country (the others had fled before the invasion) was shot.

Hussein believed that the rest of the world would sit idly by as his military marched into Kuwait. But the invasion caused an international uproar. Not only was the attack unprovoked, but Saddam's new position close to the border of Saudi Arabia, (the world's largest oil producer) was an ominous threat to all oil-consuming nations.

Almost immediately after Iraqi troops had entered Kuwaiti soil, American President **George H. Bush** imposed an economic embargo on Iraq and, backed by an international coalition of 38 nations (including many Arab countries[40]), demanded that Iraq leave Kuwait immediately and unconditionally (**UN Resolution 678**). In preparation for Bush's campaign, dubbed **Operation Desert Shield**, 230,000 U.S. troops were stationed in neighboring Saudi Arabia[41] under the command of **General Schwarzkopf** and a multi-national force of ultimately over 883,000 troops was amassed.

When the deadline for Hussein's withdrawal came and passed without any action, the allies made their move. The United State's military began conducting massive air strikes against Iraq during its **Desert Storm** offensive in January 1991, followed by a ground assault.

In an attempt to turn the allied attack into an Arab-Israeli (or East-West) conflict, Hussein tried to provoke Israel into joining the fight by firing **Scud Missiles** at them. Israeli involvement, he hoped, would turn the Arab countries (whose participation was vital for allied success) to his side. But in deference to the U.S.-led alliance, the Israelis held back retaliatory fire.

In the course of the battle, coalition forces destroyed roads, factories, electrical plants, oil refineries, transportation networks, government buildings, communications facilities, bridges and sewers leaving Iraq

---

40 Arab participants included Egypt, Syria, Saudi Arabia, Kuwait and Turkey. Jordan and Iran did not join the coalition.

41 The presence of non-Muslim troops stationed in Saudi Arabia (home to Mecca and Medina, Islam's holiest cities) was greatly opposed by devout Sunni Muslims in the Arab world (including Osama bin Laden) – despite the fact that Saudi Arabia had asked for America's help against Saddam Hussein.

Iraq in a Nutshell

dependent on foreign expertise to rebuild the country. Unable to withstand the massive assault on its infrastructure, in February 1991 Iraq agreed to a UN cease-fire and all the conditions that went along with it.

SPARING SADDAM HUSSEIN
The United States had met its objectives: the unconditional withdrawal of Iraqi troops from Kuwait, the restoration of the Kuwaiti government, and stability in the Gulf. The overthrow of Saddam, although a desirable outcome for many participants, was not the aim of the coalition attack – in part because of the involvement of Arab countries (who would have objected) and in compliance with former U.S. President **Gerald Ford's** 1976 **Executive Order #12333**, making it illegal for the U.S. to take part in assassination plots. In any case, the Americans expected Hussein's regime to collapse on its own within months under the pressure of the war and subsequent economic sanctions.

FOMENTING LOCAL CONFLICT
To hasten the process, the United States used divide-and-rule tactics and aired radio broadcasts in the country encouraging Iraqis to rise up against their defeated leader. Heeding the call, Kurds in the north and Shi'ite Muslims in southern Iraq did rebel against the dictator fully expecting the West to support their uprising. But the West did not come to their aid. Instead the U.S. allowed the defeated Iraqi army to keep its helicopters and use them against the rebels.

Although the U.S. hoped that the local unrest would accelerate the collapse of Saddam's regime, America was not prepared to commit the resources needed to maintain peace in Iraq after the dissolution of the central government. Nor was it prepared to install a new Iraqi government or prevent attacks from neighboring countries hoping to take advantage of Iraq's weakness. The U.S. decided that it was more important to curtail Iraq's ability to produce weapons of mass destruction.

RESOLUTION 687 (See Road to War, UN Resolutions pg. 111)
According to the terms of United Nations Resolution 687, Iraq was ordered to acknowledge Kuwait's sovereignty, repatriate all Kuwaitis and compensate organizations involved in repairing the country and treating casualties. Most importantly Iraq was ordered to destroy all of its ballistic missile systems (SCUDS) with a range of more than 150 kilometers (about the distance between Iraq and Israel). To ensure that the Iraqis met their obligations, weapons inspectors supervised by the

Iraq in a Nutshell

UN were deployed to monitor the disarmament process.

Faced with rebellions in the north and the south, Hussein had no choice but to agree to the United Nation's terms for a permanent cease-fire. But once the UN was satisfied, Hussein set upon the Kurdish and Shi'ite insurrectionists with such a vengeance that the United Nations was forced to set up **"no-fly zones"** prohibiting Iraqi planes from flying north of the 36 degree latitude (where the Kurds were at risk of chemical weapon attacks from the air) and below the 32 degree latitude (to protect the Shi'ites).

WAR CASUALTIES

During the course of six weeks of fighting, the Iraqis had lost about 100,000 soldiers (an unknown number were killed by allied troops as they fled Kuwait along the **"Highway of Death"**) and another 200,000 Iraqi soldiers surrendered. Tens of thousands of civilians died, including hundreds of Iraqis killed during an allied attack on a bomb shelter believed to be housing weapons. [42]

---

[42] For the first time in the history of warfare, the U.S. blasted Iraqi military vehicles with armor-piercing shells made of depleted uranium or DU. The residual emanations of the chemical left the battlefield a radioactive, toxic wasteland and is believed to be responsible for a significant increase in cancer and birth defects in the region. It may also be responsible for the mysterious illnesses suffered by Gulf War veterans (called "Gulf War Syndrome").

Iraq in a Nutshell

The allies reported 150 combat deaths, 235 non-combat deaths and 1,000 wounded during the fighting, and sources claimed that more than 100,000 American service members sent to the region during the war continue to suffer from the so-called **"Gulf War Syndrome,"** a collection of maladies including fatigue, muscle pain, memory loss, sleep disorders with no determinant cause.

SANCTIONS

Immediately following Hussein's annexation of Kuwait in August 1990, the UN imposed economic sanctions on Iraq. The sanctions continued after the conclusion of the war to pressure Iraq into complying with the demands of UN Resolution 687 and to limit Saddam's ability to rebuild his army and fund his weapons program.

The maintenance of the economic embargo became controversial after reports revealed that thousands of Iraqis (mostly children) were dying every month because of deteriorating health conditions and shortages of food and clean water. A **"food-for-oil"** provision was enacted in 1995 **(Resolution 986)** to ease the suffering by allowing Iraq to sell limited amounts of oil under strict UN supervision in exchange for humanitarian goods, but the Iraqi population continued to suffer.

International support for the sanctions diminished further when it became evident that top officials in Saddam Hussein's government (in particular, Hussein's sons) were profiting from the shortages by hoarding rationed goods and reselling them for huge profits. The regime also used the distribution of goods to serve its political agenda – for example by withholding food and medical supplies destined for Shi'ite and Kurdish areas as punishment for the post-Gulf War uprisings. According to UN experts, Saddam also smuggled millions of dollars worth of oil through countries such as Turkey and Syria and used the money to continue developing Iraq's weapons arsenal.

Although meant to put pressure on Iraq, the embargo also had a detrimental effect on neighboring countries that depended on trade with Iraq for their own economic well-being.

Iraq in a Nutshell

NEOCONS

In the 1970s, a group of hawkish liberals who saw the Vietnam War as a proxy war between the U.S. and the U.S.S.R., grew worried that the United States was reacting too passively to the threat of attack from the Soviet Union. Their concern led them to adjust their ideologies to the right side of the political spectrum, making them "new conservatives" or "neo-cons."

The early neocons (many of them Jewish) were strong supporters of Israel and felt that it was in America's best interest to make sure that the "only functioning democracy in the Middle East" survived and prospered in the midst of radical Islamists.

In addition to protecting Israel, the neocons believed that the United States had a moral responsibility as the most powerful nation on the planet to act as the world's police and to lead the international community toward political enlightenment by developing democracies worldwide. Anything less, they warned, could have catastrophic consequences.

As an example, they pointed to the fateful **Munich Agreement** of 1938 when the British and French allowed **Adolf Hitler** to take over Czechoslovakia while the United States declined to intervene. Had the Americans been more involved, they reasoned, the lives of millions of Jewish victims of the Holocaust might have been saved.

Like Hitler, Saddam Hussein had become a totalitarian dictator in the Middle East governing by terror and intimidation. Unlike Hitler, though, Hussein also possessed the near capability to produce nuclear weapons (as was demonstrated by the existence of the **Osirak** nuclear reactor). The Neocons believed he was not above passing on those weapons to terrorists.

HISTORY
When **Ronald Reagan** became the American President in 1981, the neo-cons had found a politician who shared their aggressive foreign policy. Men like **Paul Wolfowitz, Richard Perle, Frank Gaffney** and others joined the Reagan administration and participated in America's confrontation against the U.S.S.R – which, they would say later, was responsible for the eventual collapse of the Soviet Empire.

Iraq in a Nutshell

Although Reagan's successor, **George Herbert Walker Bush**, recognized and met the threat of the Baathist regime in Iraq by orchestrating the 1991 Gulf War, neocons believed his decision to allow Saddam to stay in power after the war was a vital and shortsighted mistake – one that cost the lives of hundreds of thousands of Iraqi Shi'ites, Kurds and opponents of Saddam's regime that led to the current conflict.

Instead Bush, and his successor, Democratic President **Bill Clinton** (presided 1993-2001), favored a policy of "containment" through crippling sanctions.

The election in 2000 of **George W. Bush**, a conservative Republican, gave the neocons the opportunity to reassert their authority through his administration (see box) in order to push their proactive agenda.

The terrorist attacks of September 11, 2001 demonstrated the cost of complacency against the growing threat of terrorism. It also reinforced the neocons' message that the United Stated needed to act immediately and resolutely against rogue nations, specifically Afghanistan and Iraq, – with or without the backing of the United Nations (which the neocons already felt was an ineffective and antiquated institution) or the endorsement of the international community.

NEOCONS & THE BUSH ADMINISTRATION

Dick Cheney	Vice President
Donald Rumsfeld	Secretary of Defense
Paul Wolfowitz	Deputy Secretary of Defense
Richard Armitage	Deputy Secretary of Defense
John Bolton	Undersecretary of State for Arms Control and International Security and U.S. Representative to the UN.
Richard Perle	Chairman of the Defense Policy Board
Lewis Libby*	Assistant to the President and Chief of Staff to Vice President Cheney

* Libby was later convincted for "obstruction of justice" and two counts of perjury for leaking the identity of CIA agent Valerie Plame.

Iraq in a Nutshell

Once a functioning democratic government was installed in Iraq, the neocons reasoned, the political dynamics of the Middle East would change. Palestinians, Persians, Syrians, Jordanians and other Arabs, would see the Iraqis enjoying real political, religious and economic freedom and demand the same from their own governments. The Palestinians would come down on the **Palestinian Authority** (bringing real peace to Israel), the fundamental Shi'a *mullahs* in Iran would see their authority weaken and other Middle Eastern states would witness rebellions against their corrupt regimes. In the end, the neoconservatives believed, democratic, pro-Western governments would emerge all across the traditional Islamic landscape opening up viable economic markets for western products and providing reliable strategic political allies.

Iraq in a Nutshell

ARGUMENTS IN FAVOR OF WAR (2003)

1) **Saddam was not fulfilling the promises he made at the end of the Gulf War.**
   According to UN Resolution 687, Iraq was obliged to disclose all the details of its programs to develop weapons of mass destruction and ballistic missiles with a range greater than 150 kilometers and all of its holdings of such weapons, their components and production facilities and locations. Instead, Iraq repeatedly obstructed access to sites designated by the UN Special Commission and International Atomic Energy Agency and failed to cooperate with those agencies

2) **Saddam was close to developing nuclear weapons.**
   According to experts, if Israel had not destroyed the capabilities of Iraq's Osirak nuclear facility in 1981, Hussein might have already developed nuclear weapons by the time coalition forces invaded in 1991.

3) **Iraq was capable of engaging in chemical and biological warfare.**
   UN inspectors strongly believed that Iraq maintained stockpiles of chemical agents and Hussein had proven that the regime was willing to use them.
   Iraqis had used nerve agents Sarin and Tabun as well as mustard gas and cyanide as weapons against Iranian soldiers in 1986 and against the Kurds living in northern Iraq in 1987 and 1988.

4) **Iraq could share weapons with terrorists.**
   Iraq has had links with international terrorists since the early 1970s including Abu Nidal and Carlos the Jackal. The Bush Administration suspected that Hussein also had ties with al-Qaeda, the terrorist group led by Osama bin Laden believed to be responsible for the September 11, 2001 attacks on the U.S.

5) **Human rights abuses**
   Hussein had led a regime of terror since becoming president in 1979 and had used torture and intimidation to keep the population in line.

6) **Sanctions not working**
   Hussein's family and high officials profited enormously by smuggling and reselling goods traded in the oil-for-food program that were intended to be distributed to the rest of the population.

7) **History of aggression**
   Hussein initiated both the war with Iran in 1980 and the Gulf War in 1991 when he invading Kuwait.

8) **Democracy**
   A liberated Iraq would kick-start a wave of democratization in the Middle East.

OIL

Some theorists cite Saddam Hussein's decision to begin selling Iraq's oil for euros instead of dollars ("petrodollars") in 2000 as the main impetus for the war. If other OPEC countries followed suit, the value of the dollar could have plummeted causing a deep recession in the U.S.

Iraq quietly converted back to the dollar after the fall of Baghdad.

Iraq in a Nutshell

ARGUMENTS AGAINST WAR (2003)

1) **Not legal**
   According to the UN Charter, the proposed war was not considered an act of "self-defense" and therefore not legal.
2) **Containment was successful**
   If the United States could contain a superpower like the U.S.S.R. for more than 40 years, it could continue to contain Iraq successfully.
3) **Iraq was not a direct threat to the United States**
   There was no indication that Hussein planned to use weapons of mass destruction against Europe or the United States.
4) **There was no proof that Iraq had nuclear capabilities.**
5) **There was no conclusive evidence that Hussein had any relationship with al-Qaeda or Osama bin Laden.**
   In fact, it was unlikely that the fundamental Muslim terrorist groups would have even associated with Hussein's secular regime.
6) **Little international support**
   a. Regardless of personal antagonisms against Saddam Hussein, Arab countries would feel obliged to defend their fellow-Islamic neighbor.
   b. An unprovoked invasion of a Muslim country would be considered legitimate grounds for a *jihad* (or "holy war") against the aggressors.
   c. Other countries objected to potential U.S. and British post-war dominance in the region, especially with regards to Iraqi oil.
   d. The war could add fuel to the crisis between Arab countries and the West resulting from the unresolved Israeli-Palestine conflict.
   e. A U.S. invasion of Iraq could destabilize or topple friendly governments in Turkey, Jordan, Egypt, Kuwait and Saudi Arabia.
7) **An attack on Iraq would likely increase the potential for terrorism and actually direct attention away from the war against terrorism.**
8) **Alternatives to war hadn't yet been thoroughly explored.**
   a. Sanctions could have been tightened or done away with altogether.
   b. The West could have lent more support to Iraqi opposition groups
9) **Cost of war and reconstruction.**
   a. Experts believed Britain and the U.S. would have to commit at least $20 billion a year to maintain peace in post-war Iraq and rebuild its infrastructure. *(The cost of the eight-year mission in Iraq is estimated at $1 trillion)*
   b. Without allies, the price tag would be overwhelmingly high to U.S. and U.K. taxpayers.
   c. Cost in human lives. (Nearly 4,500 American soldiers have been killed in Iraq since 2003).
10) **A weakened Iraq could be vulnerable to invasion from its neighbors (namely Iran) and become a haven for terrorists.**

OPERATION IRAQI FREEDOM
(OPERATION TELIC)

Saddam Hussein's continued violation of UN resolutions demanding free access for weapons inspectors, and the fact that sanctions weren't working provided a solid case for punitive action against the defiant Middle Eastern ruler. After the attacks in New York on September 11, 2001, the case for war escalated even higher when the Western world was suddenly forced to deal with the threat of Islamic terrorism. The assailants in the 2001 attack used planes as weapons, but the next time, it was feared, they could employ weapons of mass destruction (WMDs) or even nuclear bombs that they could be obtained from Iraq.

Saddam Hussein was known to have had contact with terrorists, notably, Palestinian terrorists **Abu Nidal** (murdered in 2002) and **Abu Abbas**, (who died two years after he was captured on the outskirts of Baghdad in April 2003), and had already used WMDs on Iranians during the Iran-Iraq War as well as on Shi'as and Kurds in his own country. His resistance to arms inspectors – who had not been allowed in the country since 1998 – gave the appearance that he had something to hide and that he could be concealing nuclear capabilities (confirmed by reports from exiled Iraqi scientists). Add to that his record of human rights abuses and his history of aggression against neighboring states and the argument for his removal by force became overwhelming.

On the other hand, his possession of nuclear arms was never proven (none were found even after troops had invaded the country in 2003) and Iraq did not pose an immediate threat to the United States or any other nation. As a secular and relatively stable country, furthermore, it acted as a bulwark against Iran (which was considered an even greater threat to U.S. security). In fact, attacking Iraq could stir up a hornet's nest of terrorist activity as Islamic militants swarmed in to defend the country from the Western infidels – as had happened with the arrival of **Abu Musab Zarqawi** and his followers. (See Sunni Insurgency pg. 87).

As the imminent war loomed, Saddam Hussein made numerous overtures to the U.S. and the U.N. Among them: presenting a 12,000 page dossier[43] disclosing Iraq's programs for weapons of mass destruction as demanded

---

43 The report was deemed incomplete by **Hans Blix**, the executive chairman of UNMOVIC, United Nations Monitoring, Verification and Inspection Commission, and other specialists.

Iraq in a Nutshell

by **UN resolution 1441** (see Road to War, UN Resolutions, pg. 111) and publicly apologizing to the people of Kuwait in December 2003 for having invaded their country in 1990.

THE ULTIMATUM

In a last-ditch attempt to avert war, the United States offered Saddam immunity from prosecution if he left Baghdad (which he refused). Two months later, the U.S. and Britain outlined a series of tasks that the Iraqi dictator should undertake or face war, including: making a public statement admitting that his country possessed WMDs and was willing to give them up; making a commitment to allow Iraqi scientists to be interviewed by inspectors outside Iraq; surrendering 10,000 liters of anthrax that he was believed to be holding; and destroying proscribed missiles, remotely piloted vehicles and mobile bio-production laboratories.

Britain, Spain, Ireland and the U.S. presented the ultimatum to the United Nations and urged its members to back military action against Iraq. In a counterproposal distributed in February 2003 though, France, Germany and Russia argued that war was premature and that effective disarmament of Iraq through peaceful means could still be accomplished. Their vetoes sealed the fate of the failed draft resolution forcing Britain, the U.S. and their allies to go it alone – in defiance even of many of their own citizens (who participated in anti-war demonstrations worldwide) [44] and governments (by March 19, 2003, nine

---

UN VOTE FOR WAR

Votes for the resolution proposed by the United States, Britain and Spain authorizing war against Iraq:

Support	Oppose	Uncertain
Britain (p)	China (p)	Angola
Bulgaria	France (p)	Cameroon
Spain	Germany	Chile
United States (p)	Russia (p)	Guinea
	Syria	Mexico
		Pakistan

("p" = permanent member)

A UN Resolution needs 9 out of 15 Security Council votes to pass. with no vote against the resolution by any of the five permanent members: United States, Britain, France, Russia and China. This resolution did not pass.

---

[44] February 15-16, 2003 saw the largest protest in history with global participation conservatively estimated at ten million people in 800 cities. The largest anti-war rally in history was in Rome with more than 2 million participants. London, Madrid and Barcelona anti-war rallies were attended by more than a million people each.

Iraq in a Nutshell

members of the British parliament had resigned in protest).

On March 18, 2003, American President **George W. Bush** gave Saddam Hussein 48 hours to leave Iraq or face invasion. The next day, 170,000 coalition troops were massed on Kuwait's border. The war began on March 20, 2003.

OPERATION IRAQI FREEDOM (March 20, 2003 – May 1, 2003)
Because Turkey had refused to allow U.S. troops to deploy from their territory, the Americans were forced to enter the country through Kuwait under the command of **General Tommy Franks**. While American troops were making their way to Baghdad, British forces were marching on Basra from the Faw Peninsula in southern Iraq. In the north, *peshmerga* fighters (armed Kurdish fighters) penetrated former Kurdish territory that had been "cleansed" of Kurds by the Saddam regime over the past 30 years.

As expected, the coalition forces enjoyed a number of victories within a few days. By April 3rd, U.S. troops captured **Saddam International Airport** (10 miles from Baghdad's city center). Three days later, British troops poured into Basra destroying the Baath party headquarters without a shot being fired. Photographs of U.S. Marines reclining in Saddam's presidential palaces gave the world a glimpse of the opulent lifestyle enjoyed by Saddam and his family while many Iraqis were living in poverty.

Most poignantly symbolic of the brutal regime's end were images of Iraqis and U.S. Marines pulling down a giant statue of Saddam Hussein in the heart of Baghdad.

In the north, meanwhile, Kurdish fighters had seized the oil city of **Kirkuk** causing the Turkish government to become concerned that victory would reignite the Kurdish bid for independence.

Saddam's final stronghold, his hometown of **Tikrit**, fell to coalition forces by mid-April.

With all the key Iraqi cities in Western hands, hostilities were formally ended on May 1,

QUSAY SADDAM HUSAYN
AL-TIKRITI
Special Security Organization
(SSO) Supervisor/Ba'th Party
Military Bureau Deputy Chairman

Iraq in a Nutshell

2003 ushering in the next phase of the war – the search for infamous Iraqi figures (identified in a pack of playing cards distributed by the U.S. military).[45]

The first of the wanted suspects to be captured was Saddam's half-brother, **Barzan Ibrahim Tikriti** who was believed to have extensive knowledge of the toppled regime's inner workings. Tariq Aziz, Saddam's former deputy prime minister, who had claimed before the war that he would rather die than become an American prisoner, surrendered to U.S. forces in Baghdad on April 24. Saddam's reviled sons **Uday** and **Qusay** (who led Iraq's elite army and security units) were killed in a gun battle in July. Ali Hassan Majid, also known as **"Chemical Ali,"** the man believed to have ordered the 1988 chemical attack on Kurds, was taken into custody on August 21, 2003.

The biggest prize, **Saddam Hussein**, was captured in December, 2003 when the gaunt and disheveled former leader was found hiding near his home town in a "spider hole" with two AK-47s and $750,000 in U.S. $100 bills.

SETBACKS

With Hussein in custody and Baghdad in the hands of coalition forces, the war had been won – but the aftermath was plagued by violence, insurgency, shortages, scandals, demonstrations and politically damaging revelations about the true status of Iraq's weapons program.

Widespread looting immediately after the war was compounded by shortages of fuel and power. Protests both in Iraq (tens of thousands of Iraqis demonstrated in Baghdad against the U.S. occupation) and in the West exhibited continued political condemnation of the war – especially after reports revealed that U.S. and U.K. intelligence had made grave mistakes regarding the extent of Iraq's possession of weapons of mass destruction and exaggerated Saddam's links with al-Qaeda terrorists.

---

45 All but ten of the original 55 "most-wanted" had been captured or killed by 2011.

Iraq in a Nutshell

When Iraqi forces surrendered to coalition forces, U.S. "pro-consul" **Jay Gardner** planned to disarm them and pay them to labor on reconstruction projects. But his replacement, Ambassador **L. Paul Bremer**, had other plans. Upon his appointment as head of the **CPA (Coalition Provisional Authority**, one of the first U.S.-led transitional governments) he disbanded the Iraqi Army, sent the soldiers home with their weapons, and fired Baath party members (virtually all Iraqi professionals). His actions caused widespread unemployment and created a cadre of disgruntled, armed former military personnel.

The morality of the occupation was called into question when graphic photos appeared in the media showing American and British guards humiliating Iraqi prisoners at **Abu Ghraib** prison – the kind of abhorrent behavior that the West was ostensibly trying to prevent by shutting down Saddam's brutal regime.

Most disheartening, though, were the prolonged battles between coalition forces and insurgents – home-grown and foreign – within Iraq. Iraqi resistance fighters who had rallied around radical Shi'as (particularly **Muqtada al-Sadr**) and violent Sunni groups (especially the group led by **Abu Musab Zarqawi**) targeted both soldiers and civilians hoping to intimidate the invaders into leaving the country. In May 2004, **Nicholas Berg**, the first in a string of Western hostages, was beheaded by Islamic militants to avenge the abuse of Iraqi detainees by US troops.

Iraq in a Nutshell

POST-SADDAM GOVERNMENTS

OFFICE OF RECONSTRUCTION AND HUMANITARIAN ASSISTANCE (ORHA) (April 21, 2003 - May 11, 2003)

Immediately after the conclusion of the war, coalition forces set up the Office of Reconstruction and Humanitarian Assistance or ORHA, a caretaker administration under the auspices of the U.S. Defense Department. Headed by retired General **Jay Garner**, who was answerable to U.S. War Commander General **Tommy Franks**, the organization was charged with providing humanitarian assistance, developing civil administration and coordinating reconstruction of post-Saddam Iraq. Along with preparing the way for the creation of a democratic Iraqi-run government, the organization was prepared to overhaul everything from the country's currency (which featured Hussein's portrait) to its legal code, schools, police service and utilities.

ORHA consisted of a core staff of about twelve people supplemented by "**free Iraqis**" – that is, Iraqis who had been living in the U.S. or Europe with no affiliations to particular Iraqi opposition groups.

The organization was renamed the **Coalition Provisional Authority** (CPA) in May 2003 and its head, retired army General Jay Garner was replaced – in part because Garner's vision of the future of Iraq differed from that of the White House. While Jay Garner supported a swift turnover of power to Iraqis, the Bush administration favored a slower transition to follow the privatization of oil and other industries.

COALITION PROVISIONAL AUTHORITY (CPA) (May 12, 2003 – June 28, 2004)

On May 12, 2003, U.S. Ambassador **Paul Bremer**, a former counterterrorism expert at the U.S. State Department, took the post of Iraq's new civil administrator, overseeing the Coalition Provisional Authority (CPA). Immediately after taking power, Bremer created a new U.S.-trained Iraqi police force, began the process of **de-Baathification** and set up an **Iraqi Special Tribunal** to conduct trials of Iraqi residents accused of genocide or crimes against humanity between 1968 and 2003.

Bremer's drive to root out all people with any association to the Baath party (as well as disbanding Iraq's military) left hundreds of thousands of Iraqi citizens without jobs and few competent administrators to serve

Iraq in a Nutshell

in Iraq's interim government. The de-Baathification policy was slowly reversed out of necessity, but not before many discontented and armed former soldiers had turned to militant organizations.

The CPA was charged with drafting a temporary constitution, appointing representatives to the United Nations and appointing interim ministers. The CPA also coordinated the transformation of Iraq's economy from a centralized planned system to a privatized free-market economy,[46] awarded contracts for reconstruction[47] and attempted to create a new Iraqi flag.[48]

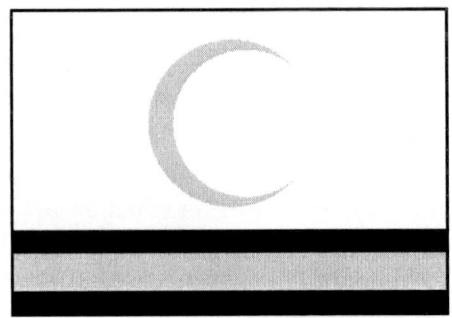

Iraqi Governing Council (IGC) (July 13, 2003 – June 2004)

A month after its creation, the Coalition Provisional Authority appointed the **Iraqi Governing Council**, a temporary Iraqi governing body subordinate to the CPA. Administrators to the diverse 25-member council were chosen by the U.S.-led coalition on the basis of population numbers. Hence the council consisted of 13 Shi'a Muslims, 5 Sunni Muslims, 5 Kurds, 1 Christian Assyrian and 1 Turkoman. Three of the members were women and none were Baathists. Nine of the Council members took turns serving as president for a month in a rotating presidential term established on July 28, 2003. The first was **Ibrahim Jaafari**, a Shi'ite spokesman for the Islamic Da'wa Party (see chapter on Shi'ites pg. 74) who served from August 1-August 31, 2003.

---

46 Critics argued that occupying forces are not legally entitled to determine an occupied country's economic model nor draft laws entitling foreign investment (another law drafted by the CPA). Proponents said the move was necessary to bring Iraq's economic law in line with that of the modern world.

47 The majority of the contracts were given to American companies such as **Bechtel** and **Halliburton**.

48 The proposed flag had a white background (standing for peace) and two blue stripes (representing Iraq's Shi'ites and Sunnis and the Tigris and Euphrates rivers) flanking a yellow stripe meant to represent the Kurds (from the color of the star on the flag of Kurdistan). A blue crescent, symbolizing Islam, floated above the lines. The flag was met with criticism by the Iraqis because it closely resembled the Israeli flag which has two light blue horizontal stripes on a white background with a Star of David in the center.

Iraq in a Nutshell

Among the members of the Iraqi Governing Council:

Iyad Allawi
A moderate Shi'ite neurologist who lived in exile in the U.K. for nearly three decades before returning to Iraq. In the early 1990s he formed the CIA-backed **Iraqi National Accord**, a dissident party determined to bring about Saddam Hussein's downfall. Allawi was later chosen by the council to be the Prime Minister of the **Iraqi Interim Government**, taking office on June 28, 2004. He was largely discredited by Iraqis as an American puppet and criticized for unpopular decisions, among them: establishing a new secret intelligence unit, the **General Security Directorate** (GSD); decreeing tough new security laws permitting the imposition of curfews and allowing emergency searches; supporting coalition attacks on Najaf and Fallujah; and banning the Arabic TV station, **Jazeera** because of its failure to support the U.S. occupation. Between 1978 and 2005 he survived three assassination attempts: the first by ordered by Saddam while he was living in England, the second (in 2004), by members of al-Qaeda in Germany and the third in the holy Iraqi city of Najaf in 2005.

Since January 2010 Allawi has headed the secular, non-sectarian **Iraqi National Movement** (known locally as **Iraqiya**) which won 91 out of 325 seats in the 2010 parliamentary election.

Ahmad Chalabi
Chalabi was a former exile and leader of the London-based **Iraqi National Council** (INC), a U.S.-funded coalition of dozens of dissident groups dedicated to Saddam's overthrow and the return of democracy to Iraq. The INC acted as an umbrella organization for Kurds, Sunnis, Shi'as, monarchists, nationalists and other dissidents dismayed with Saddam's rule. Chalabi fell from grace in the West when it was discovered that he had intentionally provided flawed intelligence to the U.S.

In 2010 Chalabi, who had been put in charge of "de-Baathification" by the Americans after the 2003 invasion, convinced the 2010 Iraqi Parliamentary election overseers to ban some 500 candidates deemed to have been too close to Saddam Hussein's Baath party in the past.

Iraq in a Nutshell

Abdul Aziz al-Hakim[49]
Abdul Aziz al-Hakim and his brother, **Muhammad Baqir Hakim**, returned to Iraq from Iran in May 2003 after 20 years living in exile. After Muhammad was assassinated in 2003 (becoming the seventh brother killed), Abdul Aziz became the leader of **SIIC**, the **Supreme Islamic Iraqi Council** (formerly the **Supreme Council for the Islamic Revolution in Iraq or SCIRI**), Iraq's most powerful Shi'a Muslim party. Abdul al-Hakim died in August 2009 in Tehran, Iran after battling lung cancer.

Massoud Barzani and Jalal Talabani
Barzani and Talabani headed the two main Kurdish groups (see chapter on Kurds) **Massoud Barzani,** led the **Kurdistan Democratic Party** (KDP) founded in 1946 by his father. **Talabani** headed the **Patriotic Union of Kurdistan** (PUK) a breakaway Kurdish party founded in 1957. On June 14, 2005, **Barzani** became the first President of the Autonomous Kurdish Government in Iraq. **Talabani** was elected State President of Iraq on April 6, 2005 and was sworn in for a second term on April 22, 2006 and a third in 2010.

Adnan Pachachi
The strongest representative of the non-Kurdish Sunni minority, Pachachi served as Iraq's foreign minister from 1965-1967 (before the Baathist's rise to power) and as ambassador to the UN (but left Iraq in 1971). In 2003, Pachachi set up and headed the liberal secular **Iraqi Independent Democrats** (which joined Allawi's coalition **Iraqiya** list in 2010). The party failed to win any seats in the 2005 legislative elections.

Aqilah Hashimi
Hashimi was one of three women on the 25-member governing council. Hashimi was shot to death in September 2003 by Iraqi insurgents targeting Iraqis collaborating with the U.S.-led administration in Iraq.

---

49 The Arabic prefix "al-" is roughly equivalent to the article "the" in English. In the case of names, "al-" denotes a description, for instance "al-Hakim" = "the wise," "al-Tikriti," meaning "the man from Tikrit." or "al-Qaeda," "the Base." The name Abdul is a contraction of "abd" ("servant of") and "al" ("the") which is often placed before one of the names of God (such as "Abd al-Aziz," the "servant of the powerful" a popular name for Allah in Islam).

Iraq in a Nutshell

Ibrahim Jaafari (Ja'afari)
Jaafari, a physician and longtime exile leader before returning to Iraq in 2003, was the spokesman for the **Islamic Da'wa Party**, one of the oldest Shi'a Islamist movements in Iraq.

Jaafari was the first in a list of rotating interim presidents after Saddam Hussein's fall. Between 2004 and 2005, he served as one of two Vice Presidents in the **Iraqi Interim Government**.

When Da'wa joined the Shi'a-dominated coalition **United Iraqi Alliance** (UIA) party, Jaafari was listed as a top candidate on the UIA ticket. The victory of the UIA in the January 2005 elections resulted in Jaafari's ascendancy as Iraq's transitional Prime Minister but because of his perceived weakness and inability to end the violence in Iraq, he wasn't reelected in 2006.

In 2008, Jaafari was expelled from the Da'wa party after forming a new political party, the **National Reform Movement** that opened talks with Da'wa rivals.

Ezzedine Salim
Salim, a former history teacher and writer, was a leader in a breakaway faction of the Da'wa party. He was killed in a bomb attack in May 2004 while serving as one of the rotating presidents in the Governing Council.

Ghazi Yawer
Yawer is a Sunni Muslim from the **Shammar tribe** – one of the largest tribal confederations in the Middle East. The Shammar, whose influence stretches from Saudi Arabia, Turkey, Jordan and Syria to southern Iraq, were supporters of the **Hashemite** monarchs of Iraq and then the **Baathist** rulers after 1958. But they lost favor when **Saddam Hussein** came to power because of their links to their Saudi Arabian tribal brothers. Ghazi was unanimously voted Interim President of Iraq under the **Iraqi Transitional Government** from May 2004 to April 2005 and became Vice President under Iraq's **Transitional Government**.

The Iraqi Governing Council was responsible for securing stability and security in the country, delivering public services and reviving the economy. It was also charged with the creation of an interim constitution or "**Transitional Administrative Law** (TAL)" (signed on March 8, 2004) which would provide the framework for the future sovereign Iraqi government.

Iraq in a Nutshell

Interim Iraqi Government (IIG) (June 28, 2004 – 2005)

The CPA and the 25-member Governing Council dissolved two days ahead of schedule on June 28, 2004 to be replaced by the autonomous Interim Iraqi Government. By transferring power early, the occupation forces hoped to catch insurgents off guard and avert any planned sabotage campaigns.

The new government was sworn in on the Quran in a small ceremony in the well-guarded **Green Zone** (see box). After shaking hands with the new Prime Minister, **Iyad Allawi,** and the ceremonial head of state, President **Ghazi Yawer**, the U.S. proconsul **L. Paul Bremer III** boarded a plane and flew home. In his place, **John Negroponte** was appointed as the new ambassador of the U.S. Embassy in Iraq, the largest embassy in the world. The IIG served as a caretaker government until national elections were held in January 2005 and a transitional government was installed.

Once in power, the IIG accepted responsibility for more than 6,000 Iraqi prisoners, including **Saddam Hussein**. The IIG also had full control over foreign relations, natural resources (including oil) and international financial negotiations. Although the IIG was allowed a single armed division of 8,000 soldiers, secu-

---

GREEN ZONE
(a.k.a. Emerald City)

Soon after coalition forces entered Iraq, they took control of a four mile area in the middle of Baghdad. The **International Zone** or "Green Zone," as it was called by military personnel to distinguish it from the dangerous "Red Zone" outside the guarded complex, enclosed streets, a large park, a convention center, villas, the Rasheed Hotel, a military museum and Saddam Hussein's Republican Palace.

After the former dictator's downfall, the new government set up shop in abandoned structures in the Green Zone and within the marbled rooms of the emptied palace overlooking the Tigris River – once Saddam's primary seat of power. Before the territory was handed back to the Iraqis, the Green Zone housed more than 5,000 government officials, private contractors and American troops who were living, shopping, conducting business and even swimming in the luxurious palace pool behind the relatively safe concrete walls.

But despite the appearance of safety, the "Green Zone" was a popular target for insurgents. The complex was shelled on a regular basis – in some months on a daily basis – causing a number of civilian and military casualties.

In January 2009, control over the International Zone was handed over to Iraqi security forces. It now houses Iraq's government offices and foreign embassies and is still the target of deadly attacks.

Iraq in a Nutshell

rity largely remained the responsibility of the coalition forces.

Upon coming to power, Allawi banned opposition militia groups including the **Badr Brigade**, then the armed wing of the **Supreme Council for the Islamic Revolution** or SCIRI (now SIIC) and the **Mahdi Army** (a paramilitary force created by Shi'ite cleric **Muqtada Sadr**). The Kurdish **Peshmerga** units were not immediately disbanded since they were needed to maintain security in northern Iraq.

While the IIG was nominally sovereign, Allawi's independent authority was doubted by many opponents who maintained that the IIG and Allawi were merely puppets of the coalition forces. Allawi's credibility might have been enhanced had he demanded the complete withdrawal of the Western/Christian forces. However, the fledgling interim government depended on coalition military services for security and American financial aid for reconstruction.

ELECTIONS January 2005

On January 30, 2005, the Iraqi people went to the polls for the first time since Saddam Hussein was deposed to select the members of Iraq's transitional parliament. The 275-member **Iraqi National Assembly** would have the task of writing a new, permanent constitution and would perform legislative functions until the constitution came into effect (at which point new elections would be held).

The voters, about 58% of the population, chose from a list of more than 100 slates (political parties) each offering a list of candidates. The number of candidates serving in the Assembly from each slate was determined by the percentage of votes the party received.

The party winning the most votes, the **United Iraqi Alliance** (receiving 48% of the vote) was allotted 140 seats. The **Democratic Patriotic Alliance of Kurdistan** was second place with 26% of the vote earning the party 75 seats. **Iyad Allawi's Iraqi List** was third with 14% of the votes and 40 seats and **The Iraqis**, the party headed by **Ghazi Yawer**, received 1.78% of the vote and 5 seats. The rest of the seats were filled by smaller parties.

Along with exercising legislative functions, the **Iraqi National Assembly** was responsible for choosing a president and two deputy presidents who would then choose a prime minister and a cabinet.
The election was largely boycotted by Sunnis, who were concerned that a

Iraq in a Nutshell

democratically elected government would favor Shi'as and Kurds. Others stayed home in fear of violence during the election process (more than 100 attacks and dozens of deaths marred the voting process). The low Sunni turnout put the legitimacy of the elected government into question.

On the same day as the national elections, Iraqis voted in local elections for leaders of provincial **Governorate Councils** and Kurds voted for members of the legislature of the **Kurdish Autonomous Region**.

PARLIAMENTARY ELECTIONS December 2005

On December 15, 2005, three months after the ratification of Iraq's permanent constitution, Iraqis went to the polls a second time to select members to serve on Iraq's 275-member **Council of Representatives** or **Federation Council** (one of two bodies of Iraq's permanent legislature).

After changes were made in the voting system granting Sunnis a more proportional representation, nearly 80% of Iraq's eligible voters risked potential violence to go to the polls.

Again voters chose parties[50] which were given seats in the parliament proportionate to the number of votes received. **United Iraqi Alliance (UIA)** (a broad-based, mostly Shi'ite coalition of 20 groups) received the most votes and was granted 41% of the seats (128). Following UIA was the **Democratic Patriotic Alliance of Kurdistan (DPAK)**, a coalition of Kurdish parties (including **KDP** and **PUK**) which received 22% of the vote and 53 seats. The **Iraqi Accord Front (Tawafuq)** (a Sunni-Islamic coalition) garnered 15% of the vote and 44 seats. And the **Iraqi National List** (a secular coalition that included Iyad Allawi's **Iraqi National Accord Party**) captured 25 seats.

After the election, a prime-minister was selected from the leading party. The winning party (**UIA**) initially chose to reelect **Ibrahim Jaafari**, the Prime Minister in the Iraqi Transitional Government, but he was forced to withdraw his nomination because of his unpopularity among Sunni, Kurdish and other groups in the parliament and his inability or unwillingness to quell rising sectarian violence and insurgency. Jaafari's tolerance of Shi'a militias, his close relationship with Iran and his connections to the firebrand cleric **Muqtada Sadr** also made him an unacceptable candidate to the United States.

In April 2006, the UIA replaced Jaafari as prime minister with Nouri Ma-

---

50 There were more than 300 official political parties and 19 coalitions registering more than 7,700 candidates. One quarter of the seats were reserved for women.

Iraq in a Nutshell

liki, a stalwart of the Dawa party who spent 24 years in exile participating in a clandestine resistance against Saddam Hussein. After his election, Maliki was given 30 days to form a national unity government that would be ratified by Iraq's parliament.

Jalal Talabani, the Kurdish leader of DPAK was re-elected as Iraq's president and **Tariq Hashimi** from primarily Sunni **Iraqi Accord Front** became vice president.

Among the new parliament's tasks: passing federal laws; approving nominees; and ratifying treaties. The **Federation Council** would also be responsible for determining policies on the distribution of oil and other natural resources, resolving the status of oil-rich **Kirkuk** (to decide whether the city would be included in the Kurdistan Region). expediting the withdrawal of Western troops, curbing the activities of the insurgents and forestalling civil war by making sure all ethnic and religious groups were represented fairly in the government.

> **ELECTION RESULTS DEC. 2005**
>
> UIA (Shi'a) 41%, 128 seats
> DPAK (Kurdish) 22%, 53 seats
> Iraq Accord Front (Sunni) 15%, 44 seats
> Iraq National List (Secular) 8%, 25 seats
> Iraqi National Dialogue Front 4%, 11 seats
> *(The remaining seats were filled by other parties)*
>
> **Prime Minister**: Ibrahim Jaafari*
> **President**: Jalal Talabani (DPAK)
> **Vice Presidents**: Adil abd Mahdi and Tariq Hashimi
>
> * *Jaafari was replaced by Nouri Maliki in May 2006.*

PARLIAMENTARY ELECTIONS March 2010

Sixty-two percent of Iraq's eligible voters went to the polls again on March 7, 2010 to decide which parties would dominate the larger 325-seat **Council of Representatives**.

The election process began with controversy when nearly 500 mostly Sunni candidates were disqualified by **Ahmad Chalabi's Independent High Electoral Commission** (IHEC)[51] for their alleged connections to the banned Baathist party, and it ended with a controversial months-long stand-off between the two narrow winners.

---

51 Ahmad Chalabi, once a favorite of neoconservatives like Richard Perle and Paul Wolfowitz, previously served as head of Iraq's Supreme National Commission for De-Baathification. The controversial Commission removed thousands of mainly Sunni-Muslim Baath Party members from their positions, including schoolteachers and other low-level officials who had become Baath party members to keep their jobs. The removals were a catalyst of the insurgency and Iraq's sectarian war.

Iraq in a Nutshell

Iyad Allawi's secular **Iraqiya National Movement (Iraqiya)** won 24.72% of the votes giving it 91 seats. The **State of Law Coalition**, a primarily Shi'a organization headed by **Nouri Maliki**, won 24.22% of the vote and 89 seats. Neither won enough votes to form a majority.

In order to bolster his support, Maliki appealed to the other Shi'a Coalition, the **Iraqi National Alliance** (INA), led by **Ibrahim Jaafari** and influenced by anti-American cleric **Muqtada Sadr**. INA had come in third in the election with 18.15% of the votes and 70 seats. Joined with State of Law and the **Kurdistan Alliance** (which had won 14.59% of the votes and 43 seats), the three coalitions dominated the government and reelected Maliki as Iraq's Prime Minister.

ELECTION RESULTS 2010

Iraq National Movement (Iraqiya List)
  24.7% of votes, 91 seats
  Leader: **Iyad Allawi**
  Secular/non-sectarian

State of Law Coalition
  24.22% of votes, 89 seats
  Leader: **Nouri Maliki**
  Includes Islamic Dawa Party
  Shi'a

Iraqi National Alliance (INA)
  18.15% of votes, 70 seats
  Leader: **Ibrahim Jaafari**
  (influenced by Muqtada Sadr)
  Successor to UIA
  Shi'a

Kurdistan Alliance
  14.59% of votes, 43 seats
  Leader: **Barham Salih**
  Includes:
    KDP (led by **Massoud Barzani**)
    PUK (led by **Jalal Talabani**)
  Kurdish

Prime Minister: Nouri Maliki (State of Law)
President: Jalal Talabani (Kurdistan Alliance)
Vice Presidents: Tariq Hashimi and Saleh Mutlaq (Iraqiya)
Head of new security council: Iyad Allawi (Iraqiya)

Iraq in a Nutshell
POLITICAL PARTIES

SHI'A PARTIES
The Shi'a-dominated **United Iraqi Alliance (UIA)**, a coalition of more than 20 groups, dominated the March and December 2005 elections. By the 2010 election, however, the coalition had broken into two lists: **Nouri Maliki's State of Law** (whose primary party was the Shi'a Islamist **Da'wa Party**); and **Ibrahim Jaafari's Iraqi National Alliance (INA)** (which was supported by followers of cleric **Muqtada al-Sadr**, Abdul Aziz Hakim's **Supreme Islamic Iraqi Council (SIIC)**, former Prime Minister **Ibrahim Jaafari** and former exile **Ahmad Chalabi**).

After the March 2010 elections the two parties joined as the **National Alliance** which supported **Nouri Maliki's** bid for a second term as Prime Minister.

KURDISH PARTIES
The **Kurdistan Alliance** is dominated by **Massoud Barzani's Kurdistan Democratic Party (KDP)** and President **Jalal Talabani's Patriotic Union of Kurdistan (PUK)**. The primary aim of Barzani (the President of Iraqi Kurdistan), Talabani and the Kurdish parties has been to advance Kurdish interests in the Iraqi parliament, protect Kurdistan's semi-autonomous status, maintain the Kurdish militia (*peshmerga*) and strengthen Kurdish control over the oil-rich city of **Kirkuk**.

The **Kurdistan Islamic Union** (KIU), which won 2% of the votes in the 2010 election and 4 seats, withdrew from the Kurdistan Alliance after the January elections. The KIU split because of the dominance of the PUK and KDP in Kurdish politics and to protest the failure of the leading Kurdish parties to reform Kurdistan's economy and root out corruption. The KIU (currently led by Sheikh **Salahaddin Bahauddin**) is the largest Islamic organization in Kurdish-controlled Iraq and maintains close ties to Egypt's Islamist **Muslim Brotherhood**.

SUNNI PARTIES
Most Sunni Muslims in the 2010 election voted for **Iyad Allawi's Iraqi National Movement (Iraqiya List)** (24.7% of the vote, 91 seats). The coalition had both Shi'a (former Prime Minister Iyad Allawi) and Sunni leaders (such as Vice Presidents **Tariq Hashimi** and **Saleh Mutlaq**) and claimed to be both secular and non-Sectarian.

Iraq in a Nutshell

The other Sunni coalition, **Iraqi Accord Front** (IAF) (which won 15% of the vote in 2005), trailed behind the Shi'a, Kurdish and secular coalitions in the 2010 election with only 2.59% of the vote winning only 6 seats. The IAF had rejected the boycott in 2005 and called on all Sunnis to participate in elections to increase Sunni representation in Iraq's parliament. The IAF's main goals: to expel U.S. forces from Iraq; end de-Baathification; and amend the constitution, especially its position on federalism.

IRAQ'S CONSTITUTION

In the referendum held on October 15, 2005, the constitution was approved by 78% of the countries voters. It was rejected by voters in the primarily Sunni Anbar province (96% of the voters said "no") and Salahuddin province (81% voted "no"). Iraqis living in Nineveh rejected the constitution by 56% just 10% shy of the required votes needed to kill it.

Among the objections:

Federalism: Sunnis were concerned that the constitution gave too much power to individual governorates (provinces) at the expense of the central government (which was intended to preserve Kurdish autonomy in the north). The Sunnis feared that the concentration of power on the local level could lead to the eventual breakup of the country leaving Sunnis living in the oil-poor center of the country deprived of profits from oil deposits in the norther Kurdish and southern Shi'a regions.

Islamism: Sunni and secular Iraqis objected to the constitution's deference to Sharia (Islamic law) as the main source of Iraqi law.

De-Baathification: Sunnis objected to constitutional provisions banning former Baath party members from higher government posts which would prevent many powerful Sunnis from serving positions of power.

Preamble
(From Associated Press English language translation)

In the name of God, the Compassionate, the Merciful,
"Verily we have honored the children of Adam" (Quran 17:70)

We the sons of Mesopotamia, the land of the prophets, resting place of the holy imams, the leaders of civilization and the creators of the alphabet, the cradle of arithmetic: on our land, the first law put in place by mankind was written; in our nation, the most noble era of justice in the politics of nations was laid down; on our soil, the followers of the prophet and the saints prayed, the philosophers and the scientists theorized and the writers and poets created.

Recognizing God's right upon us; obeying the call of our nation and our citizens; responding to the call of our religious and national leaders and the insistence of our great religious authorities and our leaders and our reformers, we went by the millions for the first time in our history to the ballot box, men and women, young and old, on 30 January 2005, remembering the pains of the despotic band's sectarian oppression of the majority; inspired by the suffering of Iraq's martyrs – Sunni and Shiite, Arab, Kurd and Turkmen, and the remaining brethren in all communities – inspired by the injustice against the holy cities in the popular uprising and against the marshes and other places; recalling the agonies of the national oppression in the massacres of Halabja, Barzan, Anfal and against the Faili Kurds; inspired by the tragedies of the Turkmen in Bashir and the suffering of the people of the western region, whom the terrorists and their allies sought to take hostage and prevent from participating in the elections and the establishment of a society of peace and brotherhood and cooperation so we can create a new Iraq of the future, without sectarianism, racial strife, regionalism, discrimination or isolation.

Terrorism and *takfir* [declaring someone an infidel] did not divert us from moving forward to build a nation of law. Sectarianism and racism did not stop us from marching together to strengthen our national unity, set ways to peacefully transfer power, adopt a manner to fairly distribute wealth and give equal opportunity to all.

We the people of Iraq, newly arisen from our disasters and looking with confidence to the future through a democratic, federal, republican system, are determined – men and women, old and young – to respect the rule of law, reject the policy of aggression, pay attention to women and their rights, the elderly and their cares, the children and their affairs, spread the culture of diversity and defuse terrorism.

We are the people of Iraq, who in all our forms and groupings undertake to establish our union freely and by choice, to learn yesterday's lessons for tomorrow, and to write down this permanent constitution from the high values and ideals of the heavenly messages and the developments of science and human civilization, and to adhere to this constitution, which shall preserve for Iraq its free union of people, land and sovereignty.

Iraq in a Nutshell

KURDS

Records of the Kurds' existence in Mesopotamia reach as far back as 3000 B.C. From the time they were first mentioned in cuneiform writing in the time of the Sumerians (as people who came from the "land of the Kardas"), Kurds have enjoyed a degree of autonomy because of the inaccessibility of the mountainous area they live in and their fighting skills.

The Kurds are a non-Arabic, primarily Sunni Muslim group of people who speak a language related to Persian (the language spoken in Iran). Traditionally they were nomadic herders organized into a number of tribal and family groups. Although today they are associated with a region called "**Kurdistan**," (which spans across parts of Iraq, Iran and Turkey), the term more accurately denotes their cultural and linguistic distinction. As drifters, the Kurds saw no need to identify with any particular geographic area until the breakup of the Ottoman Empire forced them to live within artificially designated borders.

When the British initially created Iraq from the *vilayets* of Baghdad and Basra in 1916, they did not immediately decide what to do with the Kurds living in the Ottoman Empire's former *vilayet* of **Mosul** (in northern Iraq). Like other ethnic groups at the time, the Kurds petitioned for independence after World War I and were granted their own country of **Kurdistan** in the **Treaty of Sevres**, the 1920 agreement that divided the Ottoman Empire into the modern states of Syria, Iraq and Kuwait. But the agreement was overturned by the Turks under **Mustafa Kemal Atatürk**, and

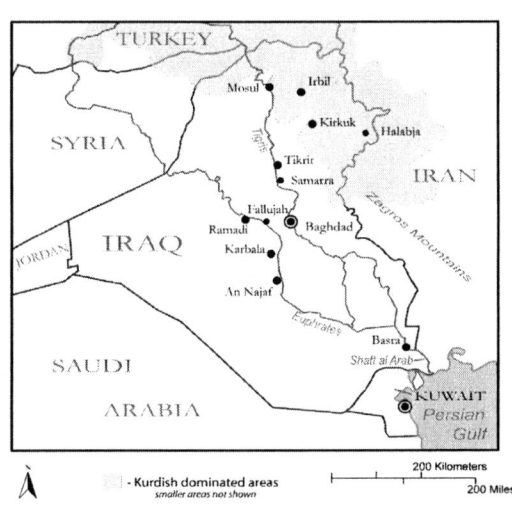

by other countries who jointly decided not to recognize an independent Kurdish state that would take territory away from their own countries.

The British were interested in maintaining control over a portion of the

Iraq in a Nutshell

Kurdish territories after it was discovered that the region had vast oil deposits. The **Treaty of Lausanne** (which superseded the Treaty of Sevres in 1923), divided Kurdistan among the countries around its borders and placed the oil-rich Mosul region within British-administered Iraq.

After 1923, "Kurdistan" and the Kurdish population were divided among five nations: the new state of Iraq (where more than four million Kurds now live, making up 15-20% of Iraq's population), Turkey (where around 17 million Kurds live, accounting for 17-25% of Turkey's population), Iran (with five to eight million Kurds, up to 10% of Iran's population), Syria (one million Kurds, 6-9% of the population) and smaller communities in Germany, Israel, Azerbaijan and other countries. Thus, the Kurds became the largest minority group in the Middle East.

Working together, the militant Kurds might have eventually succeeded in securing their own independent state. However, strong tribal and clan loyalties kept them fractured. Turkish Kurds fought Iraqi Kurds, for example, and the Iraqi Kurds were split into competing cliques.

Kurds in Iraq

One of the most prominent Iraqi Kurd groups, the **Kurdish Democratic Party (KDP),** was founded in 1946 as a political party after World War II by **Mustafa Barzani**, to oppose British influence. When the monarchy was overthrown in 1958, the KDP supported the new republican government of **Abdul Karim Kassim**, whose regime, in turn, granted the Kurds a number of liberties including the right to publish books and periodicals in their language, broadcast news in Kurdish, and use Kurdish as the language of instruction in schools.

But the rights were revoked a couple of years later when the Baathists attempted to destabilize and weaken the Kurds through a campaign of "Arabization." This included the forced resettling of Arab Iraqis in Kurdish Mosul and especially its oil-rich capital of **Kirkuk**. The Kurds, roused by the KDP, sharply resisted the Baathist campaign, turning the conflict into a prolonged battle between the Iraqi troops and the Kurds under Barzani.

In 1974, the Kurds turned to Iran for support and weapons to fight their battle of resistance against Iraq's military. But they were crushed when the Iranians, under **Mohammed Reza Shah**, promised Iraq that they would withdraw support from the Kurds in exchange for control over

Iraq in a Nutshell

the **Shatt al-Arab** waterway. (The agreement was formalized by the 1975 **Algiers Accord**). Without Iran's support, the Baathists were free to launch a devastating attack on the Kurds. Thousands of Kurdish fighters were killed as a result and some 130,000 Kurds were forced to flee to Iran – effectively extinguishing the resistance. KDP leader Barzani fled to the United States where he died a few years later.

The resistance was taken up again by another Kurdish nationalist, **Jalal Talabani**, under the banner of the **Patriotic Union of Kurdistan (PUK)** in 1976. Talabani's radical splinter group carried out Kurdish resistance from bases inside Iraq during the 1980s, frustrating Iraq's military action against Iran and its new Islamic Revolutionary leader **Ayatollah Khomeini**. (See chapter on Iran-Iraq War pg. 30.)

At the end of the Iraq-Iran war in 1988, Saddam Hussein hoped to finally eliminate the Kurdish "problem" altogether by razing hundreds of Kurdish villages in northern Iraq and killing hundreds of thousands of people in poison gas attacks. In one of the most brutal of the chemical attacks – collectively known as the "**Anfal**" campaign – Iraqi military bombers dropped missiles filled with a cocktail of chemical weapons that instantly killed thousands of Kurdish men, women and children in the border city of **Halabja**. The attacks continued from February to September 1988 under orders from Hussein's cousin, **Ali Hassan Majid** (dubbed "**Chemical Ali**").[52]

In anticipation of Iraq's defeat by the United States and allied forces at the conclusion of the 1990 Gulf War, the main Iraqi Kurdish parties (the KDP was now under the command of Barzani's sons), negotiated with Shi'ite dissidents to create a united front with the common goal of overthrowing Saddam Hussein and setting up a coalition government. Although the merger wasn't accomplished, both groups rebelled against the Iraqi regime, expecting the United States to come to their aid in support. When Western aid didn't materialize, Saddam Hussein orchestrated another wave of repression against the dissidents.

In the course of three weeks of anti-government demonstrations, thou-

---

52 "Chemical Ali" was arrested by U.S. forces in 2003 and sentenced to death in June 2007 for committing genocide and crimes against humanity. While incarcerated, he continued to defend his decision to destroy Kurdish villages on the grounds that they were "full of Iranian agents." After a few rejected appeals, "Chemical Ali" was finally hanged on January 25, 2010.

Iraq in a Nutshell

sands of unarmed civilians were executed and tens of thousands were arrested or deported. In northern Iraq, Kurds tried to escape the onslaught by fleeing to border countries, Iran and Turkey. While more than a million were accepted into Iran, Kurds amassing on the Turkish border met a different fate. The refugees were refused entry by the Turkish government and found themselves stranded in the wintry mountains without food or shelter. Thousands of Kurds died from exposure and hunger before the United States implemented **Operation Provide Comfort** – a project designed to make the Kurdish people feel safe enough to leave Turkey and resettle in their own homeland. Camps were set up with relief supplies and western troops patrolled the area. In April 1991, the U.S., Britain and France also imposed a **"no-fly zone"** across northern Iraq prohibiting Iraqi planes from flying north of the 36th parallel.

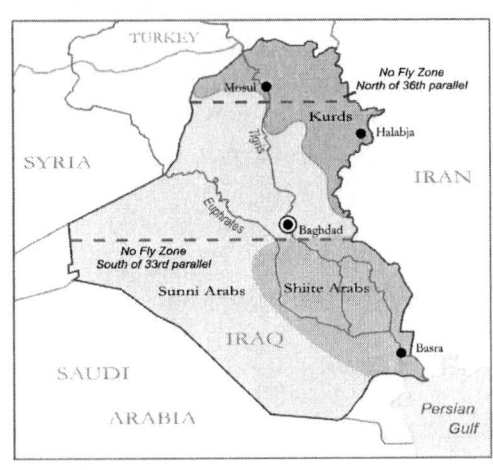

Under foreign protection, the Iraqi Kurdish community flourished. By 1992 the Kurds had established an autonomous region in northern Iraq and held general elections. Initially, power in the newly established regional government was shared by the two main Kurdish parties, the PUK and KDP. After about four years of fighting (which, at one point, led to intervention by Baghdad and other countries), the parties decided to divide the area into spheres of influence. The **KDP** (under Mustafa Barzani's son **Massoud Barzani**) would control the western region, the **PUK** (led by **Jalal Talabani**) would control the south-eastern part of Iraqi Kurdistan, and the central government would be in charge of the south.

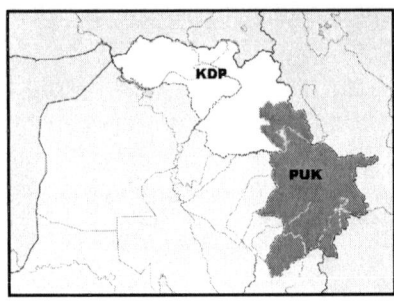

In the years leading up to the 2003 war, the Kurds enjoyed unprecedented freedoms and civil liberties. Hundreds of newspapers and magazines were published in Kurdish and other languages in the main cities, Internet access was unfettered and satellite dishes abounded. Turkmen, Assyrians and other minorities living in the area also had their own political parties and participated in the democratic government.

Iraqi "Kurdistan" had profited from commercial transit of legal and illegal goods through the area (particularly cheap oil). The Kurds also received a greater share of humanitarian items purchased under the oil-for-food program than other Iraqis.

Kurdish Flag

Despite the assertion by the Iraqi Kurds that they were not interested in establishing a greater "**Kurdistan**," the self-rule and comparative wealth raised concern in Turkey and Iran. Fearing that the region could become a base and an inspiration for separatist Kurds in their own countries, Turkey and Iran declared Iraqi Kurd sovereignty to be a potential threat to their own national security and internal stability.

Indeed, Iraqi Kurdistan did become a base for the **Kurdistan Workers Party** or **PKK**, a militant organization that has employed violence to further its aim of creating an independent, socialist, Kurdish state, and to launch attacks against Turkey. Since its creation in the 1970s, the PKK has targeted thousands of Turkish military forces and civilians, earning it the classification internationally as a terrorist organization.

When attacks increased in late 2007, the Turkish parliament voted to pursue PKK fighters militarily in Iraq – to the consternation of the U.S., which did not want to see violence spread to the only calm region in Iraq.

> **KURDISH POLITICS**
>
> The **Kurdistan Regional Government** (KRG) has been active in the Kurdistan region since 1992 and has constitutionally recognized authority over the provinces of Arbil (Irbil, Erbil), Dahuk (Dukok) and Suleimaniyah. It is currently awaiting the results of a referendum to determine whether it will also have authority over parts of Diyala, Ninevah and, most importantly, oil-rich Kirkuk.
>
> The KRG's parliament (the **Kurdistan National Assembly** or **KNA**) is headed by Prime Minister **Barham Salih** of PUK (replacing Nechirvan Barzani from KDP). President Massoud Barzani was reelected in a landslide victory in 2009 Iraqi Kurdistan elections.

Iraq in a Nutshell

In an attempt to deal with the problem diplomatically (since Turkey was seeking membership in the European Union), the Turkish government tried to press the **Kurdistan Regional Government (KRG)** to take action against the PKK itself, possibly in exchange for official recognition. Though the KRG has had its own conflicts with the PKK, it was hesitant to turn on its Kurdish brothers.

Once the war in Iraq was officially declared over on May 1, 2003 tens of thousands of Iraqi Kurds returned to lands they once occupied in the north of the country. But critics say the returning Kurds are now forcing out Arabs who were brought in by Saddam Hussein to resettle the area as part of the regime's Arabization campaign.

Much of the tension is centered on the oil-rich city of **Kirkuk**, long considered the heart and soul of the Kurdish people, where the Kurds have been accused of discriminating against Arabs.

Kirkuk

The city of Kirkuk sits on 2.2% of the earth's petroleum deposits and produces a quarter of Iraq's current output, enough to support an independent Kurdistan if it chose to break away from Iraq, and enough to bankrupt Iraq if the nation was deprived of this source of income. The status of this important city has been disputed since Saddam Hussein was ousted from power in 2003.

According to **Article 58** of the Iraqi Transitional Government constitution, measures were to be taken to "remedy the injustice caused by the previous regimes practices of altering the demographic character of certain regions, including Kirkuk" -- a reference to the Saddam Hussein's Arabization policy employed during the Anfal campaign. Steps were to be taken to "restore expelled residents to their homes or provide compensation" and to allow affected people "the right to determine their own national identity and ethnic affiliation." Iraq's permanent 2005 constitution reaffirmed the goals of Article 58 adding that a referendum be held (after normalization and a census is completed),"not later than December 31st, 2007." The citizens in the gov-

Iraq in a Nutshell

ernorate of Kirkuk and other disputed territories would determine whether or not the regions would become an inalienable part of Kurdistan.

Hoping to affect the outcome of the promised plebiscite, Kurds have "returned" to the disputed cities in droves in order to cast their votes. But the referendum was not held in 2007, or 2008 or 2010.

The incorporation of governorates like Kirkuk into Kurdistan has been sometimes violently challenged by Arabs and Turks living in the region as well as foreign countries like Turkey that fear the possible consequences for their own Kurdish minority if Kurdistan breaks away from Iraq.

Ansar Islam ("Partisans of Islam")

In 2001 various Islamic factions that had splintered from Islamic movements in Kurdistan merged to create the militant group **Ansar Islam** (initially called Jund Islam). Ansar Islam based itself in the part of Iraq that had the weakest central authority, the lawless fringes of Iraqi Kurdistan.

A month before the terrorist attacks in the United States on September 11, 2001, many of Ansar's members visited al-Qaeda leaders in Afghanistan seeking to create a base for al-Qaeda in northern Iraq. They received hundreds of thousands of dollars in seed money from the international terrorist organization before returning to Iraq ahead of the impending U.S. attack on Afghanistan after the 9/11 attacks.

Iraq's Governorates (Provinces)

1. Dahuk (Dohuk)
2. Arbil (Irbil, Erbil)
3. Suleimaniyah (Sulaymaniyah)
4. Ninevah (Nineeh, Ninawa)
5. At Ta'mim (Kirkuk)
6. Al Anbar (Anbar)
7. Salah ad Din (Salahuddin)
8. Diyala
9. Karbala (Kerbala)
10. Babil (Babel)
11. Wasit
12. An Najaf (Najaf)
13. Al Qadiiyyah (Qadisiyah)
14. Al Muthanna (Muthanna)
15. Dhi Qar
16. Maysan (Misan)
17. Al basrah (Bara)
18. Baghdad

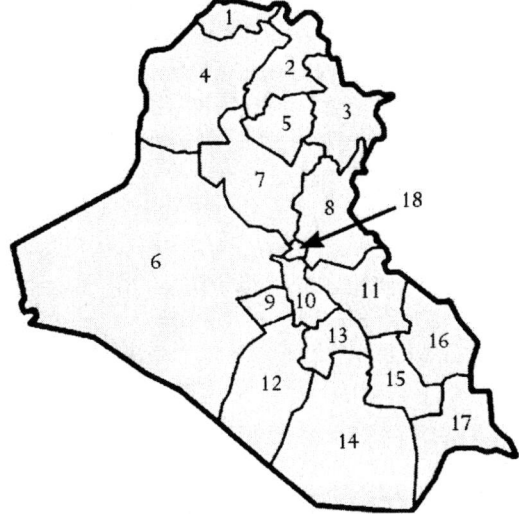

Iraq in a Nutshell

Like their counterpart al-Qaeda, the Ansar Islam group included Iraqi, Lebanese, Jordanian, Moroccan, Syrian and Palestinian fighters trained in guerrilla tactics and armed with heavy machine guns and anti-aircraft weapons. Also like al-Qaeda, Ansar leaders subjected the villagers in their hold-outs to harsh Islamic *Sharia* laws: music and singing were forbidden; girls were not allowed to attend school; women had to cover themselves in full-length *burqas* (a loose-garment with veiled holes for eyes); men were required to grow beards; and non-Muslims were required to convert, flee or be killed.

From their bases along the Iran-Iraq border (dubbed "Little Tora Bora" after the Taliban stronghold in Afghanistan), the members of Ansar aimed to expand their area of control by undermining the local administration. Their primary target was what they deemed the "blasphemous and secularist" PUK but along with capturing and killing hundreds of *peshmerga* guerrillas Ansar has also been responsible for a number acts of terrorism Ansar militants have murdered women in the streets for refusing to wear *burqas*; bombed public places (including a beauty salon and restaurant); planned political assassinations (including the attempted killing of **Burhan Salih**, head of PUK and Prime Minister of the Kurdistan Regional Government); and conducted a number of large-scale suicide attacks in Mosul, Kirkuk, Irbil and Baghdad.[53]

Although their allegiance has been to al-Qaeda, they were reportedly helped by Saddam Hussein (who smuggled arms to Ansar through Kurdish areas to try to bring down the PUK) and Iran (although Iran denies the claim).

Ansar, which recently circulated a video demonstrating their cache of rockets, silencers, IEDs ("improvised explosive devices") and remote-control automatic machine guns and full-sized cars, continues to operate from northern Iraq but has also set up recruiting centers around the world. It's original spiritual leader, **Mullah Krekar,** for instance, was operating from Norway where he was put under house arrest in 2003.[54]

The organization's military leader **Abu Abdullah al Shafi** was captured in April 2010 and sent to the controversial Abu Ghraib prison.

---

53 Ansar Islam was one of the first groups to employ women as suicide bombers.

54 Krekar, the alleged link between Saddam Hussein and al-Qaeda, trained in Afghanistan with Osama bin Laden (whom he described as the "jewel in the crown of Islam") before heading Ansar Islam. Krekar has been deemed a threat to Norway's security and an al-Qaeda collaborator prompting calls for his extradition to Kurdistan to face trial and possibly the death penalty.

MARSH ARABS

In a remote region at the confluence of the Tigris and Euphrates rivers lived a notable group of Shi'ites, the **Ma'dan** or **Marsh Arabs**. For centuries this ancient community was almost untouched by the civilizations that came through Mesopotamia, maintaining a culture based on traditional occupations of fishing, buffalo breeding and reed gathering. But the same isolation that protected the Ma'dan from invaders also made it attractive to Shi'a rebels looking for refuge from the Iraqi Baathist regime.

For this reason, and because the area had some of the richest oil deposits in the country, the Marsh Arabs were particularly singled out for repression after the Shi'ite uprisings in 1991. Thousands of Ma'dan were arrested, tortured, executed or forced to migrate, shrinking the population from about 400,000 inhabitants in the 1950s to fewer than 20,000. To facilitate entry into the area by the Baathist armed forces, the marshlands were drained – destroying one of the largest wetland ecosystems in the world.[55]

The dams that had turned the marshland into barren desert were ultimately torn down after U.S. forces invaded Iraq in 2003, slowly bringing 50% of the original marshes back to life. But though living conditions and security improved significantly, the Marsh Arabs continued to live in poverty without schools, hospitals or even clean drinking water.

Disrupted flow in water to the area (caused by prolonged droughts, global warming and upstream dams built in Turkey, Syria, Iran and northern Iraq) have also threatened the restoration of the marshes and the lives of the diverse wildlife (including migrating birds that desperately needed the watering hole for their long journey between Eurasia and Africa).

---

55 Within months the marshals were reduced to less than 10% of their original size.

Iraq in a Nutshell

TURKMEN (Turkoman)

The Turkmen make up the third largest ethnic group in Iraq after the Kurds and Arabs. Most of the nearly two million Turkmen in Iraq live in the Kirkuk and Mosul Provinces and compete with the Kurds for control of the territories. Like the Kurds, the Turkmen were victims of the Baath party's drive to Arabacize the Iraqi population by prohibiting the use of the Turkmen language in schools, the government and in public, and relocating Turkmen out of their cities and moving Arabs in.

Since Turkmen share cultural and linguistic ties to Turkey (speaking an Oguz-Turkic language), they have played an important role in the political relationship between the western coalition forces and Turkey (who has championed the cause of the Turkmen).

The Turkmens' biggest political party, the **Iraqi Turkmen Front**, founded in 1995, opposed federalism and the annexation of Kirkuk to the KRG and campaigned for a future Turkmen state. They claim that Kirkuk as well as, Irbil, Mosul and other cities are part of a larger territory of **Turkmeneli** ("land of the Turkmens") which they claim as a homeland.

Proposed borders of "Turkmeneli"

ASSYRIANS

The Assyrians are descendants of the ancient empires of Assyria and Babylonia which once ruled over Mesopotamia. Most Assyrians are Christian following the Chaldean church, Syriac Orthodox Church and the Church of the East. They suffered brutal oppression under Saddam Hussein because of their ethnicity and religion. (Christians were required to adopt Muslim names).

The Assyrians, who have never had any tribal ties, continued to be targeted by militant Muslims after 2003. Because of their Christian faith, Assyrians were perceived to have greater ties to the primarily Christian multinational forces in Iraq. Assyrian women were also targeted because they wore make-up and western-style clothes rather than the *hijab* (the Islamic headscarf).

Between December 2009 and February 2010, a particularly deadly wave of violence against the community ended with the targeted kidnappings and murders of dozens of Christians, some the victims of bombed churches. In October 2010, a bombing at the Sayidat Nejat cathedral in Mosul left 44 parishioners, two priests and seven policemen dead marking the beginning of another campaign of violence against Christians.

The attacks have prompted thousands of Assyrians to flee the Nineveh Plain to neighboring cities (more than 1,000 fled to Bakhdida, an Assyrian town in the Nineveh province). Today over 60% of the Assyrian people have fled the country or are living as refugees.

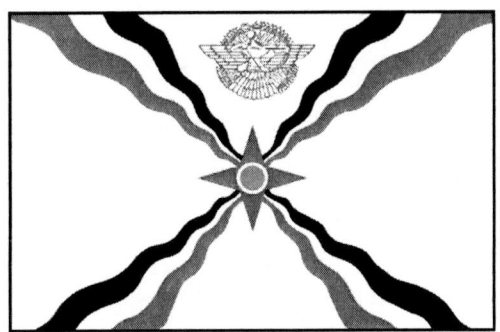

Assryian Flag

The circle in the center represents the sun. The wavy stripes represent the three major rivers of the Assyrian Homeland, the Tigris, Euphrates and the Great Zab. At the top is the image of the Assyrians pre-Christian god Assur.

Iraq in a Nutshell

SHI'ITES (SHI'AS)

Iraq is one of only three countries in the world that has a Shi'ite majority (the other two are Bahrain and Iran) and it is home to Shi'ism's most sacred shrines. But historically, the Shi'ites have been terribly underrepresented in Iraq's governments. Saddam Hussein and his Tikriti Sunni-Muslim regime ruled the religious majority with a heavy hand by imprisoning Shi'ite men, assassinating popular clerics, deporting thousands of Shi'ite women and children to Iran and keeping the southern part of Iraq (where most Shi'ites live) in a state of poverty unmatched in the rest of the country.

The split between the two Muslim groups (Shi'ites and Sunnis) began soon after the Prophet Muhammad's death in A.D. 632. The Shi'a or **Shi'at Ali** ("**Party of Ali**") believed that the Prophet's cousin and son-in-law, **Ali ibn Abu Talib**, was Muhammad's rightful successor (*caliph*) but the Muslim community chose the Prophet's close friend and supporter, **Abu Bakr**, to lead the Muslims instead. After Abu Bakr's death (and the death of two more caliphs after him) Ali was finally appointed to lead the Muslim population as the fourth caliph in A.D. 656. Five years later, Ali was assassinated and the Caliphate passed to his son, **Hassan** – but not without a fight.

Also vying for the position of caliph was **Muawiya**, the governor of Damascus, who forced Hassan to abdicate six months after his appointment and took the position of caliph himself. When Muawiya died, his son, **Yazid**, took the position, which outraged many Muslims who were offended by his excessive drinking and immoral behavior. Some disenchanted followers called on **Husayn ibn Ali,** Hassan's brother and Muhammad's youngest grandson, to retake power from the usurper.

In a celebrated battle in the city of **Kerbala** (about 60 miles southwest of Baghdad), Husayn and the outnumbered Shi'a rebels fought Yazid's forces valiantly – but couldn't stave off a massacre. According to the Shi'as,

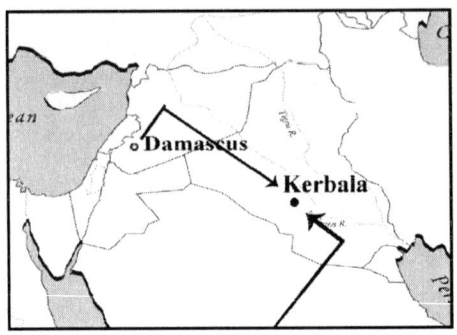

Husayn and more than 70 friends and family members were killed (or "martyred") by Yazid's soldiers on the 10th day (**Ashura**) of the Islamic month of **Muharram**. From that point on, the A.D. 680 **Battle of Kerbala** was commemorated yearly by Shi'a Muslims worldwide and pilgrimages to the

Iraq in a Nutshell

battle site and the resting places of **Ali ibn Abu Talib** (in **Najaf**) and his sons became a hallowed event.

Shi'a Muslim numbers grew considerably after the victory of the **Safavids** over Persia (Iran). The Safavid leaders (originally Sufi Muslims – a mystical branch of Sunni Islam) had converted to Shi'a Islam in the 15th century and, when they assumed power, forced the defeated populace to convert.

For the Persian Shi'a Muslims, access to the Shi'a holy sites in Mesopotamia was especially valued – and an underlying cause of many battles between the Persians and the Sunni Ottoman Turks for control over Baghdad. A few successes and failures later, the Ottomans finally won and gained control over Mesopotamia in 1638. Three decades later the Ottoman Empire collapsed and control over the three *vilayets* that would eventually make up Iraq was handed to the British.

In repayment to the Sunni-Muslim **Hashemite** family of Arabia for their help defeating the Ottomans in World War I, power over Iraq was given to **Faisal I**. By giving power over primarily Shi'a Iraq to a non-Iraqi Sunni Arab, the British hoped to appease Iraq's Sunni neighbors and ensure that Faisal would need to rely on Britain to uphold his legitimacy as Iraq's monarch. The Shi'as were virtually shut out of the puppet government of King Faisal and his successors. The Sunni **Baathists**, who equated Shi'a Islam with Iran, continued the trend of Sunni dominance.

From its earliest days, power in the Baath party remained in the hands of a narrow elite united by family and tribal ties. In order to maintain their power, the Sunni tribes elevated their tribal brothers to influential posts in the government and suppressed insurrection with an iron hand. Likewise, **Saddam Hussein** surrounded himself with Sunni Iraqis from his **Tikriti** tribe and subdued Shi'as, Kurds and non-compliant Sunnis.

In the 1970s, tens of thousands of Shi'ites were deported to diminish their numbers and influence. The numbers grew after Iran's 1979 **Islamic Revolution** (for fear that the Shi'as might become emboldened by the success of Iran's new leader, the **Ayatollah Khomeini**[56]) and especially in the course of Iraq's eight-year war with Shi'a-dominated Iran.

---

56 **Ayatollah Ruhollah Khomeini** had been living in exile in Najaf, Iraq since 1965. Abiding by a request by Iran's then-leader, **Mohammed Reza Shah**, Khomeini was expelled by the Iraqis in 1978. His rise to power in Iran after the 1979 Revolution was particularly alarming to Saddam Hussein who feared that in revenge for being expelled from Iraq, Khomeini would stir up support among Iraq's Shi'a majority and encourage them to rebel against Iraq's Sunni government.

Iraq in a Nutshell

Iran's 1979 **Islamic Revolution** was especially daunting to Iraq's Sunni government, especially considering Iraq's army was largely composed of Shi'ite soldiers. If the new wave of Shi'ite fundamentalism aroused Iraq's Shi'ites there could be a devastating rebellion. With Iranian assistance, a Shi'a uprising could topple the ruling Sunni-Muslim regime altogether. The threat was severe enough to compel Saddam Hussein to take extreme measures against the potential insurgents.

After a (possibly staged) 1982 assassination attempt in **Dujail** against Iraq's president by members of the Shi'ite resistance group, **Da'wa**, Hussein had the excuse he needed to crack down on the Shi'a community. In retaliation for the assassination attempt, 148 of the town's men were killed [57] and more than 1,000 people were tortured, imprisoned or sent to detention camps. Another half a million Shi'as were expelled throughout the 1980s under suspicions that they were sympathetic to or collaborating with Iran. (see box on following page).

Along with deportations, the Iraqi regime tortured and killed a number of Shi'ite clerics in order to deprive the Shi'ites of capable rulers and to scare other leaders into submission. The government passed discriminatory legislation against the Islamic groups, Shi'ite holy sites were desecrated, mosques, libraries and centers of learning were closed, Shi'ite religious rites and practices were restricted and printed materials were censored. The tactics worked and the Iran-Iraq war ended without a Shi'ite rebellion.

After the **Gulf War** in 1991, the Shi'ites were galvanized again to rise up against the regime – in part because they believed Saddam was no longer in power after the military defeat and because they expected the West to back them.

Initially, the revolt that had been encouraged by then-U.S. President **George H.W. Bush** was successful. Within weeks after the war's end, 15 of 18 Iraqi provinces were under the control of Shi'ite or Kurdish rebels. But the West wasn't prepared to commit its resources to a lengthy, uncertain and costly war or the country's reconstruction once the existing regime was overthrown. The American help that Shi'ite and Kurdish rebels had relied upon did not come.

Saddam's **Republican Guards** easily retook the rebel towns one by one

---

57 By killing the male head of the household, entire families would be left without breadwinners.

and unleashed a brutal wave of repression. Thousands of unarmed Shi'ite civilians were killed because of their purported participation in the insurgency and assassinations of prominent religious leaders resumed, sparking more demonstrations and, subsequently, more arrests and executions.

The physical oppression was eased after the United Nations imposed a **"no-fly zone"** at the 32 degree latitude, but as long as the Sunni Baathists controlled the distribution of rationed goods, the Shi'as were shortchanged. Iraqi government media accounts used the dire situation in southern Iraq as propaganda to show the rest of the world how much misery the *embargo* had caused in Iraq.

The Shi'ites (55% of Iraq's population) remained a formidable force in Iraq and constituted the greatest potential threat to Saddam's grip on power. After his downfall, the country's largest ethnic/religious group finally won political power equal to their numerical majority.

Execution of Saddam Hussein

Three years after he was found hiding in a hole, Saddam Hussein was put on trial for committing crimes against humanity: specifically, for the 1982 murder of 148 Iraqi Shi'ites in **Dujail** in retaliation for an attempted assassination against him. He was sentenced to death by hanging on November 5, 2006 and executed December 30, 2006.

The execution was celebrated by some Iraqis (mostly Shi'as) and criticized by others who believed he should have been tried for other crimes (Saddam Hussein is believed to have been responsible for the deaths of tens of thousands of people). Nations around the world that prohibit capital punishment condemned the United States and Iraq for administering the death penalty. There was also criticism about the undignified atmosphere during the hanging. The former President of Iraq was taunted by spectators before his death.

Saddam Hussein was buried in his hometown in Tikrit near the resting places of family members (including his sons Uday and Qusay, both killed in July 2003). Thousands of Saddam Hussein's Sunni Arab supporters regularly visit his grave to openly extol their fallen president (deemed a "hero of the insurgency"). The Iraqi government banned organized visits in 2009 after schools were arranging field trips to the site. (Public displays of paintings, statues and photographs of Saddam Hussein are forbidden elsewhere in Iraq).

SHI'A TERMS

SADR FAMILY
Grand Ayatollah Syed[58] Muhammed Baqir al-Sadr (1934? – 1980) Sadr founded the **Da'wa** Islamic Party in the late 1950s. He was executed by Saddam Hussein's regime in 1980.

Grand Ayatollah Muhammed Sadiq al-Sadr (1943? – 1999) Baqir Sadr's cousin. He was assassinated with his two eldest sons in 1999. Father of Muqtada Sadr.

Muqtada al-Sadr (1974? -) Sadiq Sadr's son. Leader of the Iraqi Islamist Sadrist Movement and head of the Mahdi Army.

HAKIM FAMILY
Grand Ayatollah Syed Muhsin al-Hakim (? – 1971) Worldwide leader of Shi'a Muslims from 1955-1970

Ayatollah Syed Muhammad Baqir al-Hakim (1939 – 2003) Son of Muhsin Hakim. Founded SCIRI (Supreme Council for Islamic Revolution in Iraq) He was killed in August 2003

Syed Abdul Aziz al-Hakim (1959 - 2009) Ayatollah Muhammad Baqir Hakim's brother. Took over as leader of SCIRI after his brother's death in 2003 He died of lung cancer on August 25th, 2009.

KHOEI[59] FAMILY
Grand Ayatollah Syed Abu al-Qasim al-Khoei (1899-1992) He was made the most prominent Grand Ayatollah in 1971 after the death of Grand Ayatollah Muhsin Syed Hakim

Syed Abdul-Majid al-Khoei (1963 – 2003) Son of Abu Qasim al-Khoei. He was assassinated in Najaf in April 2003 by Muqtada Sadr's followers.

---

58 The title "Syed," or "Sayid" in Shi'a Islam indicates that one is directly descended from the Prophet Muhammad through his daughter Fatima and her husband, Muhammad's cousin and son-in-law Ali.

59 Abu al-Qasim al-Khoei means "servant of Qasim (the first son of Prophet Muhammed who died in infancy) the man from Khoy."

Iraq in a Nutshell

GRAND AYATOLLAH SYED AL-SISTANI[60] (1930 -)
Al-Sistani is widely regarded as the spiritual leader of Iraq's Shi'a Muslims. He is currently the leader of the Hawza (seminary) in Najaf.

ISLAMIC DA'WA PARTY (IDP)
Founded in 1957 in Najaf, Da'wa's primary aim was to create a party that would promote Islamic values and ethics. The party has been led by **Nouri al-Maliki** (who was elected Iraq's Prime Minister in 2010).

SIIC or ISCI (Supreme Islamic Iraqi Council, formerly SCIRI, the Supreme Council for the Islamic Revolution in Iraq)
SIIC, an umbrella movement of Shi'ite activists, was formed by Iraqi exiles living in Iran in 1982 with the aim of overthrowing Saddam Hussein's regime. It was led by **Ayatollah Syed Muhammad Baqir al-Hakim** until his assassination by al-Qaeda terrorists in 2003. At one point, Da'wa was one of its constituent organizations but by the 1990s the two groups had developed a deadly rivalry.

BADR BRIGADE
The Badr Brigade, the armed wing of SIIC, was renamed the **Badr Organization for Development and Reconstruction** after coalition officials banned party militias in September 2003.

IRAQI NATIONAL ALLIANCE (INA) (Watani List)
INA is an alliance of Shi'a Islamic parties created by SIIC. Under the name **United Iraqi Alliance** the conservative Shi'a alliance won 128 out of 275 seats. In 2009, UIA split into the **Iraqi National Alliance** (which won 70 of 325 seats in the parliament in 2010) and the Nouri al-Maliki's **State of Law** party (which won 89 seats in 2010).

SADR CITY
A slum of two million Iraqis in East Baghdad. After the fall of Saddam Hussein's regime in 2003, the city was renamed "Sadr City" (from Saddam City) in honor of its local hero, the **Grand Ayatollah Mohammed Sadiq al-Sadr**.

MAHDI
Shi'ite Muslims believe that Muhammad's successors came from a line of descendants from Muhammad's cousin and son-in-law, **Ali**, and his wife, the Prophet's daughter, **Fatima**. **Twelver** Shi'as (the Islamic branch observed by most Shi'a Muslims in Iran and Iraq) follow the line

---

[60] The name "Sistani" comes from the Persian speaking people from the region of Sistan in southeastern Iran.

Iraq in a Nutshell

of descendants through 11 heirs or **"Imams."** They believe the last or 12th Imam (hence the name "Twelvers") disappeared into a supernatural realm and will return to prepare the way for the second coming of **Jesus** ("Isa" in Arabic) and the impending end of the world.

MAHDI ARMY The militia loyal to **Muqtada Sadr**.

NAJAF (An Najaf)
An Islamic holy city south of Baghdad. The city is the home of the shrine of **Imam Ali ibn Abi Talib,** Prophet Muhammad's cousin and son-in-law (married to Muhammad's daughter **Fatima**). It is also the site of the most sacred Shi'a Islamic cemetery. Shi'a Muslims believe that if they are buried here (near the tomb of Ali) they will quickly enter paradise. Najaf was considered the center of Shi'ite seminary education before Saddam Hussein conducted mass arrests and expelled senior clerics. (The city of **Qom** in Iran became Shi'a Islam's temporary center instead). The importance of Najaf as a hub of Islamic scholarship was restored after Saddam's fall from power in mid-2003 when scores of clerics returned to the city. During his 12-year exile, the **Grand Ayatollah Ruhollah Khomeini** lived in Najaf where he prepared to lead the 1979 Islamic Revolution in Iran.

AYATOLLAH The senior-most of Shi'a spiritual leaders. (See box below)

OBJECT OF EMULATION (Marja-i Taqilid)
The "Object of Emulation" is a popular Shi'ite clergyman – usually the foremost scholar in the shrine and seminary city, whose words and deeds are "emulated" by his followers. **Al-Sistani** and Iranian Supreme Leader **Ayatollah Ali Khamenei** are two of about seventy living Maraji (the plural of Marja).

SHI'A CLERICAL RANKS

Grand Ayatollah – Translated as "Great Sign of God"
Ayatollah – Translated as "Sign of God"
Hojat al Islam – Translated as "Authority on Islam"
Mubellegh al risala – Translated as "Carrier of the message"
Mujtahid – One who has graduated from a religious seminary
Talib ilm – Students (the Taliban, the fundamentalist Muslim group that controlled much of Afghanistan from 1995 to 2001, get their name from this term).

Advancement up the clerical ranks is based on the size and quality of one's student following and authorship of scholarly works on Islam.

SHI'ITE (SHI'A) MOVEMENTS

HISTORY OF THE ISLAMIC DA'WA PARTY
One of the oldest of the Shi'ite political parties in Iraq was founded in 1957 by **Muhammad Baqir Sadr** to establish an Islamic state in Iraq. The party was repressed by the Baathists after the Islamic Revolution in Iran in 1979 and as a response to Shi'ite demonstrations in Iraq. A year after the revolution Da'wa's founder, Baqir Sadr, was hanged and membership in the Da'wa Party was deemed a capital crime by Saddam Hussein.

After many of Da'wa's members were arrested by Saddam's regime, the party went underground and split into several factions. Iraqi Shi'ites exiled to Iran developed an Iran-based Da'wa party and others joined the party in London where they enjoyed greater freedom of movement. Members of the Da'wa party who remained in southern Iraq suffered mass arrests and executions under the Baathist regime, especially after the post-Gulf War uprisings in 1991.

After Saddam's regime was defeated in 2003, the party was re-integrated in Iraq and participated in the coalition-led **Iraqi Governing Council** and the interim government established in June 2004. In 2005, **Da'wa** joined the **Supreme Islamic Iraqi Council** (SIIC) to form the religious-Shi'ite **United Iraqi Alliance (UIA)**.

The conservative Shi'a UIA, dominated by the Dawa Party, SIIC and the Sadrist party of Muqtada Sadr, and with the blessing of **Grand Ayatollah al-Sistani**, campaigned with the promise that it would crack down on the insurgency and corruption. UIA won most of the parliamentary seats in both elections in 2005 and Da'wa's secretary-general, **Nouri Maliki**, became Iraq's first full-term Prime Minister since the fall of Saddam.

But the coalition's failure to accomplish either of its goals in its first year in office generated criticism. In early 2009, the UIA split into the **Iraqi National Alliance** (INA) led by Ammar Hakim, and the **State of Law** headed by Islamic Da'wa Party leader **Nouri Maliki**.

SUPREME ISLAMIC IRAQI COUNCIL (SIIC)
(Formerly Supreme Council for Islamic Revolution in Iraq [SCIRI])

Iraq in a Nutshell

One of the foremost opponents of Saddam's regime was **Ayatollah Muhammad Baqir al-Hakim** who founded a political group called the **Islamic Movement** in the late 1960s with **Ayatollah Muhammad Baqir al-Sadr**. Like Sadr, Hakim spent much of his life in jail for his opposition to the Baathist party.

In 1980, Hakim left Iraq for Iran where he established the **Supreme Council of the Islamic Resistance in Iraq (SCIRI)** which engaged in political activity against Saddam's regime from its Persian base. In 1991, he assumed his father's role as leader of Iraqi Shi'as, (his father, Grand **Ayatollah Muhsin al-Hakim** was a worldwide leader of Shi'a Muslims from 1955 to 1970) and in 2003, he was elevated to Grand Ayatollah.

At the end of hostilities in Iraq, Hakim ended his 23-year exile by returning to his homeland with the military arm of SCIRI, the **Badr Brigade**. With the backing of his Iranian trained and financed 10,000-strong militia, Hakim became one of the most influential Iraqi leaders supporting the Iraqi Governing Council: he drew support from and for the occupiers; he had Iranian backing; and he wielded great moral authority. It was apparently for those reasons that Grand Ayatollah Hakim was killed in a massive car bombing in Najaf in August 2003 along with dozens of other people. According to U.S. and Iraqi officials, **Abu Musab al-Zarqawi**, the militant Sunni head of **al-Qaeda in Iraq** (AQI), was responsible for the assassination.

Ayatollah Hakim's brother, **Syed Abdul Aziz Hakim** took over as leader of the SCIRI and the Badr Brigade and served as Interim President of the Iraqi Governing Council in December 2003. In 2005, he was a top candidate on the **United Iraqi Alliance (UIA)** list in the January elections.

In May 2007, **Supreme Council for Islamic Revolution in Iraq (SCIRI)** formally changed its name to **Supreme Islamic Iraqi Council (SIIC)** – dropping the word "Revolution" to reflect Iraq's new political atmosphere.

ABU QASIM AL-KHOEI
After the death of **Grand Ayatollah Muhsin al-Hakim** in 1971, the role of **Object of Emulation** was passed to **Abu Qasim al-Khoei.** Like many of his fellow Shi'ites, the Grand Ayatollah was arrested after the Gulf War and placed under house arrest. After his death in 1992, the Shi'as were split in their allegiances between the older generation who followed **Khoei's** disciple, the **Grand Ayatollah al-Sistani,** and the younger gen-

eration, who were drawn to the younger activist scholar **Muhammad Sadiq al-Sadr**.

GRAND AYATOLLAH AL-SISTANI

After the death of **Grand Ayatollah Abu Qasim Khoei**, many Iraqi Shi'ite Muslims recognized the spiritual leadership of his disciple, the Grand Ayatollah Sistani. Born in the Iranian holy city of Qom and educated in Najaf, Sistani was influenced by his mentor, Khoei, and adopted his conviction that religion and politics should not be mixed. By keeping a low profile in the political sphere, he was able to survive Saddam Hussein's repression against Iraqi Shi'ites and develop a strong theological base of supporters.

When the U.S.-led forces invaded Iraq, al-Sistani continued to keep his distance from the conflict and urged his followers to do the same by not taking arms against the occupation force. From the first month after the war, Sistani was courted by the West because of his moderate views in spite of his open ambition to impose an Islamic identity on post-Saddam Iraq, and even after the cleric criticized U.S. political decisions.

As Ayatollah, al-Sistani was in charge of millions of dollars donated by Muslims worldwide to support the religious education of future Islamic scholars and he has exerted great spiritual authority over the Iraqi Shi'a population. Politically, he rejected the Iranian model of theocracy and favored separation of church and state. He has refused to endorse political parties, though it has been widely accepted that he tacitly endorsed the **United Iraqi Alliance**.

GRAND AYATOLLAH MUHAMMAD SADIQ SADR

While many of the older, conservative Shi'a Muslims followed al-Sistani's religious leadership after the death of the senior al-Khoei in 1992, the younger Shi'ites chose to assemble around the fiery young cleric, **Ayatollah Muhammad Sadiq al-Sadr**, cousin of the martyred Islamic theorist, **Muhammad Baqir al-Sadr**. Sadr and his loyal followers – most of whom were from the slums of East Baghdad ("**Sadr City**") where al-Sadr had established charitable institutions and a network of mosques– were vocal opponents of Saddam Hussein and often rioted against the Baathist regime (particularly in 1977 and 1991). Sadr's boldness eventually led to his assassination by Saddam's secret police in 1999.

Iraq in a Nutshell

MUQTADA SADR

Muhammad Sadiq Sadr's son, **Muqtada Sadr**, took over where his father left off – although only in his late twenties, the younger Sadr lacked the religious training required of the highest-ranking Shi'ite leaders. Muqtada Sadr based his authority on his lineage which included his father, the martyred Shi'ite cleric **Ayatollah Muhammed Sadiq Sadr** and his uncle, the **Ayatollah Muhammad Baqir Sadr** (the leading Shi'ite activist killed by Saddam's forces in the late 1980).

His power base came from his inherited network of supporters from Sadr City and other Shi'ite Iraqi towns. Drawing on his father's **Sadr Foundation**, Muqtada and his followers distributed food and supplies around Baghdad's suburbs in the first weeks of the 2003 invasion and reopened mosques once the fighting had stopped.

In June 2003, the fiercely anti-U.S. Shi'ite cleric established a militia group called the **Mahdi Army** to help bring about the enforcement of Islamic Law in the country. Believed to command 3,000 to 10,000 guerrillas, the Mahdi Army was named for the hidden Imam that Twelver Shi'ite believe will appear in messianic form during the last days of the world. Sadr had convinced his supporters that the Americans had come to Iraq to subdue the Shi'ites and prevent them from establishing a Shi'ite religious government in Iraq. As an alternative to the U.S.-dominated Iraqi Governing Council and its successor, the Interim Iraqi Government led by Allawi, Sadr proposed establishing a shadow government based on Islamic principles and ruling by Sharia law.

Sadr also set up a weekly newspaper called **Hawza** that was shut down by the coalition authorities at the end of March 2004 on charges that it lied about U.S. attacks on the Shi'as and incited anti-U.S. violence. In response, Sadr mobilized his supporters to protest the closure in a number of Iraqi cities. By the beginning of April, peaceful protests turned violent, engaging the coalition forces in gun battles in Najaf, Sadr City and Basra.

A few months later, Sadr again called on his followers to rise up and fight U.S. troops (who had surrounded his home and exchanged fire with members of Sadr's militia). On August 5th, Sadr's Mahdi Army attacked a Najaf police station, triggering intense clashes between Sadr's supporters and U.S. forces throughout the city's revered sites, primarily the

Iraq in a Nutshell

Imam Ali shrine and the adjacent cemetery. The standoff continued until August 25, 2004 when Ayatollah Sistani negotiated a cease-fire agreement on his return to Iraq after having had surgery in London.

Like other clerics, Muqtada did not actively participate in the 2005 elections. It is believed that he tacitly supported the National Independent Cadres and Elites party though many of his supporters backed the UIA (favored by Sistani). That changed after 2009.

Between 2007 and 2010, while Sadr was studying in the religious city of Qom[61], the rebellious Shi'a cleric became more and more determined to play a greater role in Iraqi politics. In his effort to gain legitimacy, Sadr distanced himself from militia violence and focused on charity. His political muscle was deeply felt during the six-month-long stalemate after the 2010 elections between Iyad Allawi's secular Iraqiya party and Nouri Maliki's State of Law. By lending his support to Maliki[62] (in exchange for powerful ministries promised to the Sadrists), Sadr guaranteed Maliki's accession to power.

Despite his temporary renunciation of violence, Muqtada Sadr remained virulently anti-American, openly pledging to unleash the fury of his Mahdi militia if the U.S. troops didn't leave Iraq by the 2011 deadline.

RIVALRIES

Conflicts among the SCIRI, the Sadr bloc, Da'wa and the followers of Grand Ayatollah Ali Sistani were historically driven by the struggle for control over key Islamic sites – principally, the shrines of Imam Ali in Najaf and that of his son Husayn in Kerbala.

Sadr vs. Khoei

In April 2003, Abu Qasim Khoei's son, **Abdul Majid Khoei** – who had just returned to Iraq from exile in London – was stabbed to death at the Imam Ali shrine in Najaf along with the shrine's controversial caretaker. The murder was believed to have been carried out by Muqtada Sadr's supporters (the Sadrists or Sadriyun).

Sadr vs. Ayatollah Muhammed Baqir Hakim

The Sadr family and the Hakim family both vied for authority over the

---

61 Sadr fled to Iran in 2008 after Prime Minister Maliki crushed Sadr's Mahdi army in south Basra. He returned to Iraq in early 2011.
62 Sadr's faction commanded 40 seats in the Iraqi parliament.

Iraq in a Nutshell

Iraqi Shi'ite community. In August 2003, Ayatollah Baqir Hakim was killed along with 84 other people in a massive bomb attack at the Imam Ali Mosque. Sadr was among those accused of the murder – although U.S. and Iraqi officials determined that the suicide bomber was associated with Sunni militant **Musab Zarqawi**.

Sadr vs. Sistani

The murder of **Abdul Majid al-Khoei**, the son of al-Sistani's mentor, fueled the animosity that had been simmering between the moderate cleric, Sistani, and his radical rival, **Muqtada al-Sadr**. Politically, al-Sistani believed that Shi'a clerics should limit their guidance to religious issues and stay out of politics. Conversely, al-Sadr called for the establishment of a shadow government and popular resistance to the occupation. As Grand Ayatollah, al-Sistani managed millions of dollars in donations from pilgrims and wealthy donors which al-Sadr coveted. Sadr also raised objections about Sistani's "foreign origin," implying that Sistani's connection with Iran made him unfit to wield influence in Iraq.

On some occasions, the rivalry over control of holy sites resulted in armed clashes between al-Sadr's Mahdi Army and al-Sistani's Badr Army.

Sadr vs. Maliki

When Nouri al-Maliki became Prime Minister in 2005, he had a political obligation to break his alliance with the rebellious cleric, Muqtada Sadr. Sadr, himself, also objected to the government's close relationship with the West. In February 2006, Sadr urged dozens of his followers in Iraq's parliament to protest Maliki's meeting with U.S. President George W. Bush. The rift between the Prime Minister and Shi'a cleric deepened with the escalation of sectarian violence and ethnic cleansing in Baghdad by Sadr's Mahdi Army.

In reaction to the violence, and under U.S. pressure, al-Maliki vowed to confront all armed groups (a thinly veiled threat to the Mahdi Army). Maliki's crackdown resulted in a national army strike at Sadr's militia in Basra (prompting Sadr to flee to Iran) and the arrest of hundreds of the firebrand cleric's followers.

In light of the Sadrist-Maliki rancor, it came as a surprise to many when the Muqtada al-Sadr decided to support al-Maliki's reelection as Prime Minister in 2010.

Iraq in a Nutshell

SUNNI INSURGENCY

The fall of Saddam Hussein brought about the end of a brutal dictatorship. And his demise also resulted in an end to the 80-year old domination of the Iraqi state by the Sunni Arab minority.

SUNNI DOMINANCE
The hegemony of the minority Sunnis began even before the creation of Iraq during the Ottoman Empire when Sunnis were prominent in the administration of the provinces of Baghdad, Basra and, to an extent, Mosul. When the British took over after World War I, they understood the importance of Sunni dominance as a counter to the Shi'a-dominated state of Persia (renamed Iran in 1935). With the installation of Sunni monarch **King Faisal I** on the Iraqi throne, Sunni authority was sealed until the fall of Saddam Hussein's regime in 2003 and the U.S.-coalition drive to establish democratic rule.

The new **Coalition Provisional Authority** allotted most of its 25 administrative seats to the numerically greater Shi'a Arabs (13 seats) while the non-Kurdish Sunnis received only six seats (Kurds were allotted 4 seats, Assyrians and Turkmen had one seat each).

UNEMPLOYMENT
In the aftermath of the 2003 invasion of Iraq, the new U.S.-led government took great measures to strip all Iraqis who had been associated with Saddam Hussein's Baathist government of their power. In the course of the subsequent **de-Baathification** drive, thousands of primarily Sunni-Muslim civil servants (reportedly including about 28,000 teachers) were fired. At the same time, about 450,000 soldiers were demobilized without pay or pension – but in possession of their weapons. Iraq's military had been a refuge for poor young men in the first half of the 20th century and its fighters had been on almost continuous active duty since Iraq's war with Iran beginning in 1980. It is estimated that more than 2 million people had been dependent on pay received from the military.

Other victims of the defeat of the Baathist regime were tribal leaders who had received favors from Saddam Hussein in an attempt to extend his influence to the villages. Tribal practices and loyalties dominated in the area of the **Sunni Triangle** (see box on pg. 88) where traditional expressions of pride and revenge fueled the Sunni insurgency against

Iraq in a Nutshell

the foreign invaders – especially among Iraqis who had lost friends or family members in the fighting.

The West had long been held accountable for the despair and poverty that resulted from twelve years of sanctions. After the 2003 war, the British and Americans were also blamed for the interruption of basic public services (electricity, water and sewage), critical unemployment and lawlessness that beleaguered the country after fighting had ended.

Iraqi suspicions that coalition forces had entered the country in order to pillage Iraq's resources provoked insurgents to sabotage the oil industry by bombing pipelines and other facilities. In fact, one of the first tasks of the U.S. forces after entering Iraq in 2003 was to protect oil facilities so that local parties couldn't take control of key oil production installations to gain political leverage in post-war Iraq.

SUNNI TRIANGLE

Area stretching west from Baghdad to the town of Ramadi and north to Tikrit, including Fallujah

Of concern to Islamists[63] within Iraq and neighboring countries was the possibility that the Christian invaders were intent on abolishing Islam. Following the trend in the rest of the Muslim world, the Islamic revival in Iraq had been flourishing after decades of suppression. Even Saddam Hussein recognized the political advantage of upholding the Islamic faith. In 1991, the previously secular president of Iraq attempted to demonstrate his piety by adding the words "**Allahu Akbar**" ("God is great") written in his own handwriting to Iraq's national flag.

Iraq's flag 1991-2004

SALAFIS
Most insurgent Islamist Sunni Iraqis follow the austere "Salafi" or

---

63 Islamists are conservatives Muslims who believe that Islam is not only a religion but a political and a social system. They believe Muslims should return to their Islamic roots and unite against non-Muslims.

Iraq in a Nutshell

"Wahhabi"[64] branch of Islam practiced in Saudi Arabia. Salafis insist on a literal interpretation of the Quran (Islam's holy book) and advocate returning to the pure Islam of the time of Prophet Muhammad. They were particularly opposed to foreign and non-Muslim influences on the religion and many saw their battle against the "Christian" troops of the coalition forces as a "holy war" (*jihad*). For the Sunni Muslim clerics of **Fallujah** (also called the "City of Mosques" because its estimated 300,000 residents are known for their piety) the invasion presented an opportunity to impose **Sharia** (Islamic law) – especially after U.S. Marines gave up control of the city to a local militia. (see box on Fallujah, pg. 92)

FOREIGN FIGHTERS

The Iraqi cause also attracted *mujahideen* (Islamic holy warriors) from Syria, Jordan, Saudi Arabia, Egypt, Sudan and Chechnya who took up the insurgency against occupation forces with violent results.

Among the most dangerous and capable player in this group of foreign fighters was **Abu Musab Zarqawi**, a Jordanian-born militant with ties to al-Qaeda. Zarqawi headed an insurgency group called **Al Tawhid Awl-Jihad** ("Monotheism and Holy Struggle") which became "al-Qaeda in Mesopotamia" or popularly, "**al-Qaeda in Iraq (AQI)**." The organization, which became active in Iraq after 2003, was responsible for numerous kidnappings, beheading and suicide bombings in Iraq – including the February 22, 2006 bombing of the **Askari Mosque**.

ASKARI MOSQUE (February 22, 2006 and June 13, 2007)

The Askari Mosque in the town of Samarra (Salah ad-din province) is considered one of the holiest sites in Shi'a Islam. It houses the remains of the 10th and 11th Imams (the Shi'a Islamic line of successors of Prophet Muhammad through his cousin Ali and daughter Fatima) and is built adjacent to the shrine of the 12th or "**Hidden Imam**" (who Shi'as anticipate will return to earth at the End of Times to usher in a just and perfect Islamic society).

The golden dome of the shrine was bombed on February 22, 2006, reportedly by Sunni insurgents associated with al-Qaeda in Iraq. The attack, along with another bombing in June 2007 that destroyed the mosque's minarets, did not result in any deaths but sparked a firestorm of sectarian

---

64 The name "Wahhabi" is considered derogatory by the Salafists since it implies that they revere the founder of the fundamentalist Islamic branch, **Muhammed bin Abd Wahhab**. For more on the Salafis please see Roraback's Islam in a Nutshell, Enisen Publishing, 2010.

Iraq in a Nutshell

revenge strikes. Sunni Mosques were targeted by Shi'as provoking retaliatory assaults by Sunnis. Many Muslims from both faiths (including Muqtada Sadr, Iranian Supreme leader Ayatollah Ali Khamenei, Kashmiri Indians, members of Shi'a groups in Bahrain etc.) blamed the Americans for the destruction – either directly, because they failed to protect the holy shrines, or because their presence in Iraq had provoked sectarian violence. Many high-profile Iraqis (like Sistani and Abdul Aziz Hakim) urged Shi'as not to take revenge on Sunni Muslims for the attack while Sunni tribal leaders asked their members to restrain from targeting Iraqi Shi'as.

AL-QAEDA IN IRAQ (AQI)

After Abu Musab Zarqawi was killed in a U.S. military airstrike in June 2006, leadership of AQI was passed to **Abu Hamza Muhajir.**[65] The goals of the terrorist organization were to expel U.S. forces from Iraq, assassinate collaborators with the occupation, reestablish the Islamic Caliphate, and destroy Jewish dominion over Israel/Palestine. In January 2006, AQI tried to lend local legitimacy to their cause by inviting Iraqi Sunni *jihadists* (those who fight a "**jihad**" or "holy war" in the name of Islam) under the banner of the **Mujaheddin Shura**. The organization was not successful. In fact, many Iraqi Sunni tribes who had become disgusted with the violent tactics of AQI eventually collaborated with the United States to combat the foreign fighters.

Although AQI accounted for just a fraction of insurgency violence in Iraq, it was considered the most dangerous. Operating under the shadow of the insurgent umbrella organization, **Islamic State of Iraq** (ISI), (headed by **Abu Omar al-Qurashi al-Baghdadi**[66] until 2010), AQI employed guerilla-style tactics – kidnappings, beheadings, planting of improvised explosive devices (IEDs), attacks using rocket-propelled grenades – to target foreign journalists, U.S. military personnel, Iraqi security forces, Iraqi politicians, Shi'a militias and hundreds of Iraqi civilians.

On the Shi'a holy day of Ashura (memorializing the day Prophet Muhammad's grandson Hussein was killed by Yazid) in 2004, AQI was responsible for a series of bombs in Baghdad and Kerbala (leaving more than 150

---

65 **Abu Hamza Muhajir** (literally "Father of Hamza the immigrant") and **Omar Baghdadi** were killed near Tikrit in April 2010 in a joint American and Iraqi operation. There was evidence on the computers seized from Muhajir's complex that the terrorist had exchanged e-mails with both Osama bin Laden and his deputy Ayman Zawahiri (both also dead).

66 Until his reported death in April 2010, there was speculation that Omar Baghdadi was in fact a fictitious figure conjured up to give an Iraqi face to the foreign (non-Iraqi)-dominated group.

people dead). The same year, they abducted a number of foreigners including American businessman **Nick Berg** whose decapitation was captured on video and circulated on the internet.[67]

Beginning in 2006, under the banner of the ISI, Sunni insurgents took credit many of Baghdad's bombings (including the 2010 bombing of a church during a Sunday Mass in 2010) killing and injuring hundreds of Iraqis.

ANBAR AWAKENING

In September 2006, Abdul Sattar Buzaigh Rishawi, a prominent Sunni tribal leader from the city of Ramadi in the Anbar province, founded the **Anbar Awakening** (or Anbar Salvation Council), an alliance of dozens of Sunni tribes who had turned against insurgents linked to al-Qaeda. The organization collaborated with their former enemies, the Shi'ite-led Iraqi government and the Americans, to coordinate attacks against al-Qaeda extremists in the Sunni-dominated **Anbar province**. The U.S. and Iraqi governments supplied the Sunni tribal members with weapons, ammunition and cars. In turn, the members of Anbar Awakening told the Americans where the extremists were hiding weapons, burying bombs and running safe houses while setting up road blocks and engaging in gunfights with al-Qaeda *jihadists*.

ANBAR PROVINCE

A vast area extending from the Syrian border to the western outskirts of Baghdad. (see province map on pg. 41)

SURGE 2007

Emboldened by the victory in Anbar, U.S. President G. W. Bush announced that the U.S. would deploy more than 20,000 additional American troops to Iraq. The troops, under the command of General **David Petraeus**, were sent to Baghdad where they would help Iraqi forces clear and secure neighborhoods, and to the primarily Sunni Muslim Anbar province where al-Qaeda terrorists had amassed.

By the end of the year, violence had sharply decreased in Iraq, in part because of the "clear-and-hold" tactics of the new American troops and because of the Awakening movement. The decrease in al-Qaeda bombings against Shi'a targets resulted in fewer retaliatory strikes giving local militias less reason to operate. In August 2007 as a result, the militant **Mahdi Army** loyal to **Muqtada al-Sadr** declared a cease-fire.

---

67 On the video the kidnappers said the beheading was, in part, in retaliation for the indignities on Muslim men and women at Abu Ghraib prison.

Iraq in a Nutshell

The pacification of the most dangerous neighborhoods in Iraq helped inspire U.S. President Bush to announce the withdrawal of thousands of troops from Iraq by 2008.

FALLUJAH (Fallouja, Falluja)
Anbar Province

Thirty to forty miles west of Baghdad, Fallujah was a hotbed of Sunni-led resistance against coalition forces. The city's residents were known for their religious piety: women, in the rare occasions that they were seen in public, covered themselves from head to toe; liquor stores were banned; and men sported beards in observance of Islamic tradition.

A year after the occupation, the city had become a staging ground for indigenous insurgents and foreign extremists (including many Qaeda operatives) engaged in the "holy war" against the infidel west.

On March 31, 2004, Iraqi insurgents attacked a convoy containing American private military contractors from **Blackwater, USA** (see pg. 65) as it passed through Fallujah. The insurgents killed four armed contractors from the convoy and mutilated their bodies. Jubilant crowds were seen dragging the charred corpses through the streets of Fallujah before they were hung from a bridge spanning the Euphrates. Chilling images of the event circulated through the internet and were leaked to American news agencies generating disgust and outrage in the United States.

In response, coalition forces led a counteroffensive against the insurgents. After a three-week siege, the U.S. handed authority over the city to a local militia called the **Fallujah Brigade** commanded by a former Saddam-era general.

The handover was locally deemed a victory against the occupiers and the ineffectual Fallujah Brigade (now disbanded) could not prevent the reassertion of power by hard-line Islamic leaders.

Strict Sharia law was imposed on the residents upon the departure of the U.S. troops and a local Islamic court was installed to administer Islamic punishments for local crimes (hands were cut off for theft, 80 lashes were given for selling alcohol etc.).

For the next few months, American and Iraqi forces concentrated their efforts on pacifying the city. The Fallujah insurgents were largely subdued by the end of the year. But in the course of the fighting, hundreds of insurgents and dozens of American soldiers died and thousands of homes were destroyed.

U.S. WITHDRAWAL FROM IRAQ

The success of the 2007 Surge, the impending end of the UN Security Council resolution that had allowed the temporary presence of military forces in Iraq,[68] the U.S. presidential debate,[69] general public opinion and other factors prompted U.S. President **George W. Bush** and Iraq's Prime Minister **Maliki** to begin negotiating the end of America's military presence in Iraq.

George W. Bush had entered the talks hoping to gain legitimacy for a long-term military presence in Iraq but Maliki and the Iraqis, reeling from the killing of 17 Iraqi civilians by gunmen hired by the private security firm **Blackwater, USA** (see pg. 94) came to the table with a more aggressive agenda.

After a year of hard bargaining, it was agreed that American troops would pull out of most Iraqi cities by the summer of 2009 and would leave the country, leaving no permanent bases, by the end of 2011 unless requested to stay by the Iraqi government.

The **Status of Forces Agreement (SOFA)** was officially signed by the Iraqi Foreign Minster and U.S. Ambassador Ryan Crocker on November 17, 2008 and was ratified by the Iraqi Parliament ten days later.

Along with the promised withdrawal of troops, the Status of Force Agreement required U.S. troops to have Iraqi judicial warrants for searches of homes and buildings not related to combat and forbade the practice of detaining people over 24 hours without government approval. While contractors working for the State Department and other U.S. agencies maintained their immunity, U.S. contractors and off-duty, off-base U.S. soldiers[70] would be subject to Iraqi criminal law. The United States also

---

68 UN Resolution 1511 passed in October 2003 stated that the internationally recognized status of the occupying powers (Britain and the U.S.) would cease when an internationally recognized representative government was established by the people and sworn in.

69 Then-Democratic presidential candidate **Barack Obama** was running on a platform promoting a timeline for U.S. withdrawal (within 16 months of taking office).against Republican candidate **John McCain** who favored a conditions-based timeframe for withdrawal. The Iraqis preferred Obama's plan.

70 Perhaps the first case of Americans facing Iraqi justice took place in 2009 when five Americans were arrested for killing an American contractor in Baghdad's Green Zone. In October 2011, when it became clear that American military trainers might be needed in Iraq after the deadline, Iraq's political leaders declared that any troops remaining after 2011 should not be granted immunity from Iraqi law. The issue of immunity has been particularly controversial in light of abuses like the Abu Ghraib prison scandal and Blackwater killings.

Iraq in a Nutshell

agreed not to attack Iraq's neighbors from inside Iraq (a provision intended to persuade allies of Iran in the Iraqi government to support the agreement).

On August 19, 2010 the last U.S. combat brigade withdrew from Iraq leaving about 50,000 non-combat US. troops who would act as advisors. By this point, "Operation Iraqi Freedom," the name given to the U.S.-led Coalition military operations against Iraq in March 2003, was replaced by "**Operation New Dawn.**" The remaining U.S. servicemen would conduct stability operations and work on training Iraqi Security forces from bases outside major Iraqi cities until the prescribed departure time.

BLACKWATER, USA
(Renamed "Blackwater Worldwide" in 2007)

On September 16, 2007, seventeen Iraqi civilians were killed by employees of the private security firm, Blackwater U.S.A while the contractors were escorting a convoy of U.S. State Department vehicles through Baghdad. The incident brought the organization and U.S. reliance on private companies into the limelight. The Iraqi government wanted to try the Blackwater security guards in Iraqi courts but, due to Order 17 signed by Paul Bremer while he presided over the Coalition Provisional Authority (CPA), contractors were immune from the Iraqi legal process. American laws regarding contractors operating in Iraq and Afghanistan also exempted Blackwater employees from prosecution by the U.S. government.

Blackwater Worldwide is one of dozens of companies hired by the U.S. State Department to provide everything from food service to the troops and reconstruction expertise to security for diplomats (as Blackwater was hired to do). The numbers of private contractors are not generally counted among occupation or casualty counts skewing the extent of America's involvement in the region and the number of American victims of violence in Iraq. The cost for contractors (often recruited from among veterans of the Iraq war) can also exceed sixfold the salary of a U.S. soldier.

The Iraqi government revoked Blackwater's license to operate in Iraq after the shooting, and a month later, the U.S. House of Representatives passed a bill that would make all private contractors working in Iraq subject to prosecution in U.S. courts. But controversy continued to brew over America's reliance on private firms (deemed "mercenaries" by some) to assume responsibilities including security, training etc. on the battlefield.

MAJOR ISSUES

The Status of Forces Agreement stipulated that American troops were to leave the country by the end of 2011 unless invited to stay by the Iraqi government. With U.S. troops gone, however, Iraq would be left to deal with a number of unresolved internal issues.

CORRUPTION
In 2004, an auotonomous body was created to promote the rule of law in Iraq. The independent nature of the **Commission on Public Integrity**, as the body was called, was formalized in the 2005 Iraqi Constitution. But, because of intimidation and limitations placed on the organization, it has done little to eradicate the rampant corruption that has plagued the country.

According to Transparency International, a non-governmental organization that monitors and fights worldwide corruption, Iraq was ranked the fourth worst country in the world for corruption in 2010, behind only Burma, Somalia and Afghanistan.

With violence waning in the country, corruption has become one of the Iraq's foremost problems and a great obstacle to the country's development.

Corruption has tainted almost every level of the society from teachers, doctors, clergymen and police to senior ministry officials. Iraqis know that no job is awarded without a bribe and that advancement depends on greased palms. Even movement around Iraq involves payment for passage through checkpoints (which had initially been set up to stop insurgents). The checkpoints have become so lucrative, in fact, that they are being sold for tens of thousands of dollars.

In upper levels of government, ministers have raked in millions of dollars by embezzling from the country's $2 billion a week oil revenues (which could otherwise go to fund municipal services like electricity and trash collection), skimming "fees" collected from U.S. reconstruction funds and accepting bribes from crooked businessmen. (This on top of the $9,000 a month salaries[71] and generous perks and pension plans earned by Members of Parliament).

---

71 Because of the wages and the high cost of the security detail (which can require dozens of bodyguards for each MP), it reportedly costs the Iraqi government about $30,000 a month to employ one Member of Parliament..

Iraq in a Nutshell

The widespread corruption has eroded public trust in the government and has resulted in dangerous consequences. A cholera epidemic that broke out in several places in 2008, for example, was reportedly caused by contaminated drinking water because an Iraqi official accepted a bribe to buy chlorine from Iran that was long past its expiration date. (The official was released from jail shortly after his arrest because of his connections to SIIC). In other cases, dangerous terrorists have been released from jail after paying sizable bribes.

The activities of the Commission on Public Integrity, which was created to prevent this kind of corruption, has been impeded by the government since its inception. Maliki's government has been accused of undermining the commission by depriving it of funding, blocking access to government departments and harassing the Commission's employees. When the watchdog agency testified in Washington that the Iraqi government had embezzled $13 million in American reconstruction funds, Maliki fired the monitors. Other employees of the Commission have been murdered in the line of duty.

The weakness of the Commission was clearly demonstrated in September 2011 when the agency's chief, **Judge Rahim al-Ugaili**, was forced to resign after investigating alleged corruption among government officials – the same day the popular radio journalist **Hadi al-Mahdi** was killed in Baghdad.

The attempt to silence potential whistle-blowers has been part of a growing trend of violations of basic human rights.

CIVIL RIGHTS

Along with guaranteeing the independent activities of the Commission on Public Integrity, Articles 38 and 42 in the 2005 Constitution guarantee freedom of expression, freedom of the press, freedom of assembly and freedom of thought, conscience and belief. Since 2003, foreign correspondents have been able to write freely about Maliki's foibles (including his decision to fire corruption monitors) but the liberty has not been extended to the local media.

Although Iraq's ranking in the **Press Freedom Index** has improved since 2005, it still ranked in the bottom third in 2010 (130th out of 173 countries). In order to keep reports of corruption and incompetence out of the country's press, Iraq's government has exerted great pressure on the press through criminal charges, suspensions and harassment by Iraqi security forces. In the worst cases, journalists have been silenced through attacks, kidnapping and murder.

The popular outspoken radio talk show personality **Hadi al-Mahdi**, the host of a program called **"To Whoever Listens"** which was highly critical of the government,[72] was forced to take his show off the air for fear of retribution. On September 9, 2011, before he was to lead a pro-democracy demonstration against corruption and authoritarianism, al-Mahdi was shot in the head at his home in an otherwise safe neighborhood in Baghdad.

Ironically, a month earlier Iraq's government had adopted a law that was intended to "promote the rights of journalists and ensure their protection within the republic of Iraq."[73]

Another example of Iraq's slide back to the Saddam era of civil rights abuses has been the increasing number of unlawful detentions and physical abuse of political enemies. Torture (including hanging prisoners upsidedown, subjecting detainees to electric shocks and pulling out fingernails) has become routine in government detention centers. Some of the worst offenders are members of an elite unit of 3,000 Iraqi soldiers known as the Brigade 56 or **Baghdad Brigade**. The special force (derisively called the "dirty squad") reports to the Justice Ministry (according to Iraq's deputy justice minister) or directly to Prime Minister Maliki (as claimed by Human Rights Watch), and has been accused of holding detainees accused of terrorism for months at a time without a trial.[74]

Without American oversight, some fear the infringement of freedoms and brutal practices of Security Forces portend the return of a police state in Iraq.

MUNICIPAL SERVICES

For most Iraqis, a more pressing problem has been the lack of basic mu-

---

[72] In May 2010, the New York Times reported that Mahdi, deemed the "Rush Limbaugh in Iraq" reportedly ridiculed the government's decision to disqualify Sunni candidates in the March 2010 elections, criticized corruption in the universities and lambasted Prime Minister Maliki and the "dirty Parliament." His show reached 4% of Iraq's population.

[73] Reporters Without Borders has criticized the law for being too vague and containing too many serious omissions to be effective.

[74] The international non-governmental organization Human Rights Watch has reported the existence of a number of secret jails in the heart of Baghdad where detainees are held in inhumane conditions and subject to violent interrogations.

Iraq in a Nutshell

nicipal services. After decades of war and sanctions, Iraq's infrastructure was in shambles before the 2003 invasion.

Before the war, the supply of electricity was just 7,900 megawatts. The levels have increased since then (due to billions of dollars in American investments) but the demand has more than doubled due to new access to air conditioners, refrigerators, washing machines and other power-hungry electronics. In 2011, few areas across the country could get more than 3 or 4 hours of electricity a day, some regions could only count on an hour or two.

Although better than during Saddam times, the lack of electricity was still bad enough to provoke deadly uprisings in Basra and other parts of the country in the summer of 2010 (when temperatures rose above 120° F (50° Celsius) and in 2011, when Iraqis, inspired by successful demonstration in Libya and Tunisia, marched in the streets again calling for improved public services.[75]

The shortage of energy is the result of seven years of violence, fuel shortages at power stations, corruption, the political deadlock in 2010, criminal activity, vandalism and desperate and greedy Iraqis who illegally tapped into the already overwhelmed electrical grid. Because electricity is so inexpensive, moreover, there is little incentive to conserve it. Instead, some Iraqis have invested in expensive Diesel or gasoline generators (although, due to nationwide gasoline shortages, acquiring fuel for the generator can require standing in line for hours at gas stations).

The lack of electricity has had a number of consequences. People are afraid to leave their house at night for fear of thieves and thugs roaming the unlit streets. Sweltering summers without air-conditioners and drinking water have resulted in cases of dehydration and heatstroke. Without electricity, moreover, water treatment and sewage plants could not operate.

The collapse of the sanitation infrastructure in Iraq and the disruption in waste collection[76] have also become a major health hazard.

---

[75] After the "Electricity Uprising" in 2010, the Ministry of Electricity resigned and Maliki ordered the emergency lines to the Green Zone and the homes of the state's officials cut. He also said that it would take about two years to negotiate contracts with Siemens and General Electric to build the country's power grid.

[76] Garbage collecting has become one of the most dangerous jobs in Iraq. Hundreds of waste collectors have been killed while attempting to pick up garbage in violent neighborhoods. There is also a chronic shortage of garbage trucks.

Iraq in a Nutshell

BUSINESS
Another victim of Iraq's lack of electricity and corruption has been the country's business and industrial sector.

Iraq sits on the world's second largest oil reserves which provides 95% of the country's revenue. But the oil industry employs only 1% of the population.

Because of the country's reliance on oil revenues and because of Saddam's focus on wars (the 1980-88 Iran-Iraq War and the 1991 Gulf War) Iraq never adequately developed its industry. Since Iraq has not produced many of its own goods, Iraqis have relied on imported consumer products. During the embargo enacted by the U.S. against Saddam Hussein's regime, most goods in the shops came from China. After 2003, the stores were flooded with Western and Iranian products – but still few locally produced goods.

In the last few years, existing Iraqi businesses have had to overcome many obstacles in order to keep their enterprises afloat. Without electricity, proprietors have been forced to buy expensive generators to keep machines running, lights illuminating and to keep perishables from spoiling. Buying fuel in bulk, though, could require getting written permission from half a dozen government departments (each expecting kick-backs to push the process along). Still more money was spent to transport goods and materials through the various checkpoints in the country.

Starting a new business had its own challenges. Banks charged up to 20% interest on small loans and could demand 300% in collateral to guarantee the loan. Foreign investors who haven't been scared off by reports of violence (which Iraqis have complained has been exaggerated in Western media), are turned off by the corruption. Large investors choose instead to do business in the safer, more modern regions in the semi-autonomous Kurdish north. In surveys by the World Bank, Iraq ranked near the bottom in terms of ease of starting a business (175th out of 183 countries).

The lack of industry and businesses has resulted in unemployment (16% in 2011) leaving millions of young men out of work and dangerously desperate and vulnerable to recruitment in questionable pursuits.

FOREIGN INTERFERENCE
As Americans prepared to leave Iraq when the impending December 2011 deadline approached, the race for geopolitical influence in the re-

Iraq in a Nutshell

gion escalated. Iraq's neighbors, Turkey, Saudi Arabia, Iran and Syria, have been angling for greater influence lest the vacuum left by departing troops be filled by a regional rival.

The Turks, fearful that Kurdish power in northern Iraq could encourage Turkish Kurds to seek independence in Turkey, have worked to minimize Kurdish autonomy, especially in the oil-rich region of Kirkuk. Turkey also hopes that Iraq will soon become Turkey's main export market. Already Turkey has become a visible presence in pop culture and shops, which carry many Turkish goods. The Turks have invested heavily in Kurdistan (more than half of all foreign businesses in Iraqi Kurdistan are Turkish). Turkey also plans to help Iraq build roads, airports, oil and gas pipelines such as the major oil pipeline that runs from Kirkuk to Ceyhan in Turkey that carries a quarter of Iraq's oil exports.[77]

And Saudi Arabia and Iran have played out their long-term religious and political rivalry in a proxy war in Iraq.[78]

Iran's influence in Iraq has vexed Americans who maintain sanctions against the Shi'ite-Muslim nation for fear of its potential to build nuclear weapons. But Iran has made deep inroads over the border, religiously, politically and militarily. Many of Iraq's leaders, including Prime Minister Maliki[79] and Iraq's religious leader al-Sistani, spent many years in exile in Iran. And when access to the Shi'ite religious cities of Najaf and Kerbala in Iraq opened up after Saddam Hussein fell from power, hundreds of thousands of Shi'a-Muslim Iranians poured into the country to visit the holy sites.

---

[77] Turkish firms have been busy refurbishing the Sheraton Hotel in Basra, building the International Fair Grounds and planning multiple flights a week from Istanbul to Basra. Turkish ships also supply the city of Basra with electricity.

[78] Sunni-Muslim-dominated Saudi Arabia, the birthplace of Islam and the Arabic language, has long considered itself the vanguard of the "true path" of Islam against heretical Shi'as (championed by Shi'a-Muslim Iran which considers itself culturally superior to Saudi Arabia). Since the 1979 Islamic Revolution in Iran, Saudi Arabia has worked to check Iran's rise while Iran has worked to increase its influence in the Middle East as the advocate of a pan-Islamic alliance against imperialists. Both nations have also come to blows over oil: Saudi Arabia, the largest producer of oil, has favored a lower price of oil ($70 to $80 a barrel), Iran, sitting on the Middle East's second largest oil deposits, prefers a higher price. The zero-sum rivalry has played out in a number of proxy battlefields including Iraq, Bahrain, Lebanon, Syria, Palestine, Yemen and other regions where there is potential sectarian rivalry or concerns about foreign influence.

[79] Turkish voters in Iran, who supported Maliki's rival Ayad Allawi in the March 2010 elections, considered Nouri al-Maliki an Iranian puppet and strongman intent on exercising near dictatorial powers.

Iraq in a Nutshell

Like Turkey, Iran has also seen Iraq as a valuable trade partner and has flooded the shops in southern Iraq with Iranian goods.[80] To facilitate Iran-Iraq trade and tourism, the Persian nation has constructed roads linking Basra with Iranian commercial centers across the border, an airport in Najaf and made plans to build a branch of its national bank in Baghdad. Southern Iraq, in fact, has become the only place outside of Iran where the Iranian currency, the *rial*, is used.

Iraq historically has been Iran's western line of defense against foreign invasion. To keep that buffer zone secure, Iranians have also worked to ensure the rise of a powerful, Iranian-friendly government and weaken rival-American "colonists." To that end, Iran has been accused of supplying Shi'a insurgents (like the Badr Brigade) with explosives, rockets, training and intelligence.

Saudi Arabia did not join the Coalition that toppled Saddam Hussein for fear that Iraq would fracture along sectarian lines and threaten the Sunni-Arabian nation. After 2003, Riyadh kept a worried eye on Iraq's Shi'a-dominated government and the growing influence of Iran in the country. The Saudis are concerned about the future of Iraq's domestic stability and oil production policies which could directly affect Saudi Arabia, the world's largest oil exporter.

---

80 Exports from Iran to Iraq topped $1.8 billion in 2006.

Iraq in a Nutshell

THE POLITICS OF OIL

At the turn of the century, **Winston Churchill**, then-British Secretary of State for War and Air, decided to convert the Royal Navy from a coal burning to an oil-burning fleet to gain advantage over the Germans. Since then Middle Eastern oil has played a powerful role in world politics.

Britain, which had no oil of its own, was forced to get the commodity abroad and, like the French, Germans, Russians and Americans, set its sights on the oil potential in the Middle East.

Initially, Britain tapped into newly-discovered oil in Persia by forming the **Anglo-Persian Oil Company** (which became **British Petroleum**). When an entrepreneurial Armenian, **Calouste Gulbenkian,** calculated that oil must also exist underneath the deserts of Mesopotamia, Britain jumped at the opportunity and united with Germany and the **Royal Dutch-Shell Company** to create the **Turkish Petroleum Company** (TPC) in 1912.

The drive for oil intensified a few years later when nations fighting in **World War I** (1914-1918) recognized the importance of oil for military purposes (to fuel naval ships, tanks, trucks, submarines and even military airplanes), and then faced a petroleum shortage.

By 1918, Britain had staked its claim on the potentially oil-rich Ottoman *vilayets* of Baghdad and Basra and was working to secure administrative control over **Mosul** (which had been promised to France under the secret **Sykes-Picot** agreement that carved-up the Ottoman Empire). The French, who lacked oil themselves, were offered Germany's quarter share in TPC as consolation, along with French dominance over Lebanon and Syria.

The Anglo-French agreement enraged the Americans, who insisted that they, too, be given a share in the Oil Company. To accommodate the U.S., a year after oil was discovered in **Kirkuk** in northern Iraq (1927), American companies **Jersey Standard** and **Socony** (**Exxon** and **Mobil**) were allotted a 23.75% stake in TPC.

But while the British, French, U.S. and even Gulbenkian (who received a 5% share in TPC and became one of the richest men in the world) all profited from Mesopotamian oil, the Iraqis received nothing until they took matters into their own hands.

Iraq in a Nutshell

IRAQ TAKES CONTROL OVER ITS OIL RESERVES

In 1958, all the members of the British-backed Royal Iraqi branch of the Hashemite family were brutally killed in a military coup led by **General Karim Kassim**. Iraq's new government immediately demanded vast revisions in the concessions of the TPC (now called the **Iraq Petroleum Company** [IPC]) and in the early 1960s revoked 99.5% of IPC's concessions.

Later in the year, Iraq helped create the **Organization of Petroleum Exporting Countries** (OPEC) to help its five founding members (Iraq, Iran, Kuwait, Saudi Arabia and Venezuela) – the sources of over 80% of the world's crude oil exports – exercise complete sovereignty over oil production. Although initially OPEC did little for its member countries, the organization later fulfilled its objective by coordinating and unifying petroleum policies in order to establish fair and stable prices for petroleum producers. In 1973 OPEC created the **"petro-dollar"** by only accepting the U.S. dollar in payment for oil, ensuring worldwide demand for the dollar and offsetting the U.S.'s trade imbalance.

After Kassim's murder in 1963, the incoming Baath Party established the **Iraqi National Oil Company** (INOC) to exploit the areas that had been expropriated from IPC's European members a couple of years earlier.

After the 1967 Arab-Israeli war, which resulted in strong anti-American and anti-British sentiments throughout the Arab world, Iraq began to turn to other countries to help them develop their oil industry, in particular, France and the Soviet Union. Money borrowed from these countries to pay for the exploration and development of their oil fields was to be repaid in crude oil when the oil wells were functional.

In 1972, the Baath Party under **Ahmed Hassan Bakr** (Iraq's President from 1968 to 1979) repealed the remaining 0.5% of IPC concessions giving Iraq 100% control over its own oil industry. The Iraqi regime used the new oil revenues to fund domestic infrastructure projects, develop transportation projects and make other improvements in the country. **Saddam Hussein**, who played a prominent role in Bakr's government, saw his own popularity rise as Iraq prospered, facilitating his ascension to the presidency in 1979.

Iraq in a Nutshell

OIL AND THE IRAN-IRAQ WAR (see Iran-Iraq War pg. 30)
With Iraq's wealth tied to its oil trade, it was imperative to secure the nation's main export routes, including the **Shatt al-Arab waterway** (Iraq's only water access to the Persian Gulf). But the war that Hussein initiated against Iran to secure control over the waterway also interrupted the flow and transport of the nation's most valuable resource. After eight years of war, Iraq's oil industry was in shambles – oil wells had been neglected or destroyed in war, the rest of the world had turned to other countries for their petroleum supplies and Iraq's economy was too weak to rebuild the oil industry infrastructure. To make matters worse, the world price of oil had dropped precipitously by the late 1980s making economic recovery even more difficult.

OIL AND THE GULF WAR (See Gulf War, pg. 33)
Saddam blamed Kuwait for most of the country's ills. He accused the Kuwaitis of stealing from the **Rumaila** oil field (which was shared by the two countries) and flooding the oil market thereby driving down prices. In retaliation, he declared war against the small nation in 1990.

Rather than easing Iraq's economic crisis, though, the war against Kuwait only made matters worse. Sanctions imposed by the UN at the onset of the war blocked the country's oil-trade and the terms of subsequent UN Resolutions put Iraq's oil industry virtually back into foreign hands (in particular **UN Resolution 706** in August 1991 which stipulated that all profits from petroleum sales from Iraq be put into an escrow account to be administered by the Security-General of the UN). Without money to maintain oil wells or explore new sources, Iraq's production levels continued to drop much lower than the country's potential.

Hoping to sway UN voting nations into campaigning for the lifting of economic sanctions, Hussein attempted to woo countries like France, Russia and China by promising them lucrative oil deals if and when sanctions were dropped.

With a greatly diminished petroleum output and stiffly regulated export restrictions, Iraq had been eliminated as a source of competition by other oil producing nations. Consequently, Saudi Arabia, the world's largest producer of oil in the world, (Iraq is the second) became such a dominant oil exporter that nations feared it held an inordinate amount of leverage over world oil prices and supplies. Any move to withhold oil sales by Saudi Arabia for political or ideological reasons could result in economic havoc. Opening up Iraq's oil trade, on the other hand, would again balance the playing field.

Iraq's high-quality oil is the cheapest to produce and experts believe that the country has been sitting on billions of barrels worth of untapped oil reserves. As long as Saddam Hussein was in power and the sanctions were continued, that potential would remain untapped.

Although U.S. President **George W. Bush** and his administration insisted that oil was not a factor in his decision to go to war with Iraq, the issue remained at the forefront of international debate. In 2000, Saddam Hussein stopped accepting the dollar in payment for oil in favor of the euro, a move that was reversed when the U.S. invaded Iraq in 2003. OPEC and especially Iran also considered converting from petrodollar to **petroeuros**, a move that would devalue the U.S. dollar and depress the U.S. economy.

The United States and Britain (the biggest proponents of war against Iraq), stood to profit greatly when Hussein was unseated from power giving them access to oil fields that were earlier restricted. At the same time, France, Russia and China lost contracts that had been signed with the Iraqi dictator years ago to develop new oil fields and rehabilitate existing ones once UN sanctions were lifted.

Iraq in a Nutshell

WEAPONS OF MASS DESTRUCTION (WMDs)

Just as vast oil reserves made Iraq economically powerful, the possession of weapons of mass destruction, the regime reasoned, would make Iraq militarily and strategically powerful in the Middle East, especially as a defense against potentially belligerent neighbors such as Iran, Turkey and Israel (which has its own nuclear weapons).

But as a participant in the **Nuclear Non-Proliferation Treaty (NPT)** and under the provisions of a series of UN Security Council Resolutions, Iraq was legally prohibited from producing and maintaining any weapons of mass destruction. The use of chemical warfare, moreover, had been strictly outlawed since the Geneva Protocol was ratified in 1925.

Iraq's blatant disregard for the international prohibitions gave the country a reputation for being a dangerous rogue nation.

NUCLEAR WEAPONS
Iraq began its civilian nuclear program (developing nuclear energy for non-military use) in 1956 when it acquired readily-available documents from the U.S. patent office outlining details of the **Manhattan Project** (the West's first atomic weapons project). In 1962, the plans were used to begin construction on Iraq's first nuclear research reactor.

In 1968 Iraq signed the Nuclear Non-Proliferation Treaty – a treaty that obliges its members to forgo the manufacture of nuclear weapons and submit its nuclear materials and facilities to regular inspections by the **International Atomic Energy Agency (IAEA).** In return for cooperation, NPT member countries received access to nuclear technology and were entitled to have an active reactor as long as it was used for peaceful purposes. Iraq, an oil-rich nation with no apparent need for an alternative energy source, took advantage of its membership in the NPT to cultivate its own nuclear weapons program.

By infiltrating the IAEA (Iraqi scientists were installed in the organization to learn its methods and promote Iraq's interests), the Iraqi regime was able to hide its weapons program from the NPT and the world. Meanwhile, teams of scientists (including **Khidir Hamza**, Saddam's self-proclaimed "bomb maker" who exposed details about Iraq's nuclear

Iraq in a Nutshell

program after defecting to the U.S. in 1994) scoured foreign countries for parts and materials for its ostensibly "peaceful" nuclear agenda.

Under the noses of the inspectors, Iraq initiated the country's first illicit uranium enrichment project and, in 1974, the country legally purchased a research reactor from France (named **Osirak** by the French and redubbed **Tammuz I** by Iraq). Despite Hussein's confession in an Arabic-language news magazine that Iraq wanted to be the first Arab nation to engage in nuclear arming, the only foreign country that was alarmed enough to take measures (having used French reactors to built its own nuclear arsenal) was Israel.

In June 1981, Israeli pilots dropped thirteen bombs on the new French reactor core, demolishing Osirak (Tammuz) and setting back Iraq's nuclear program by years. Some experts believe that had the Israelis not targeted Tammuz, Hussein might have had functional nuclear weapons by the time he invaded Kuwait in 1990.

After secretly pursuing a multi-billion dollar nuclear weapons program, Iraq's nuclear potential was curtailed again after the country's defeat in the 1991 Persian Gulf War. In compliance with the cease-fire agreement (as outlined in **UN Security Resolution 687**), the United Nations created a **Special Commission (UNSCOM)** to inspect Iraq's weapons facilities and monitor the country's disarmament.

By the time UN inspectors began their work in Iraq in the 1990s, the regime had already mastered the art of deception – having hidden prohibited weapons production from the IAEA for years. From the UN Commission's creation in 1991 until inspectors were deported from Iraq in 1998, Hussein and his regime played a cat-and-mouse game with UNSCOM by blocking entrances to various facilities, claiming to have destroyed some weapons and denying the production of others.

Despite repeated attempts to sabotage UNSCOM's investigation, UN workers quickly discovered and monitored the destruction of stockpiles of chemical and biological weapons and dismantled facilities built to produce them. Inspectors also discovered that Iraq had been producing enriched fuel for atomic weapons and, by studying thousands of confiscated documents, learned how far along Iraq's weapons development program actually was.

Iraq in a Nutshell

The greatest disclosure, though, was made by Saddam's son-in-law General **Hussein Kamel Majid** who had been in charge of Iraq's weapons programs. Fearing the ruthless temper of Saddam's son, **Uday**, Kamel Majid and his brother defected to Jordan in 1995 where they revealed intimate details about Iraq's weapons program. Consequently, the Iraqi regime was forced to admit it still possessed a cache of weapons of mass destruction that had been overlooked by the inspectors. The brothers were executed for treason by Hussein's henchmen after they returned to Iraq.

By 1998, Hussein, recognizing that compliance with the inspections would not guarantee the lifting of sanctions, decided to put an end to UN activity. Claiming that American inspectors were spies for the CIA, Hussein first announced that the U.S. would no longer be allowed to participate in UNSCOM activities. Then, on August 5, 1998, he unilaterally cut off inspections altogether.

U.S. President **Bill Clinton**, (who was in the middle of impeachment hearings) threatened to bomb Iraq if Hussein didn't readmit inspectors immediately. Brief military action in December 1998 (**Operation Desert Fox**) was followed by an offer to the Iraqi president – if Hussein fully complied with renewed inspections for nine months (UNSCOM was to be replaced by the **UN Monitoring, Verification and Inspection Commission [UNMOVIC]**), economic sanctions would be lifted. Hussein refused the deal claiming that Iraq was hiding nothing. Intelligence reports, however, demonstrated that Hussein had continued to assemble an arsenal of weapons of mass destruction while the inspectors were gone. British intelligence reports claiming that Iraq had tried to smuggle significant supplies of uranium from Nigeria, Africa were questioned by nuclear inspectors and refuted by U.S. Ambassador **Joseph Wilson IV** when he was sent by the Bush administration to Nigeria to verify it. In retaliation, the Bush administration illegally revealed that Ambassador Wilson's wife, **Valerie Plame**, was a CIA agent, resulting in the trial and conviction of then-Vice Presidential aid **Lewis "Scooter" Libby**.

CHEMICAL AND BIOLOGICAL WEAPONS

Unlike nuclear weapons, which can cost millions of dollars and require specialized technological expertise, chemical and biological weapons are easy to make, easy to transport, easy to use and easy to hide. A chemical or biological attack, furthermore, can cause as much damage as a nuclear bomb – killing thousands of people with a single assault.

Iraq in a Nutshell

Iraq began to research these types of weapons in the 1970s. By the time war broke out against Iran in the 1980s, Hussein's regime was able to produce a number of chemical agents including mustard gas, CS tear gas and **tabun**. When the Iran-Iraq war turned against Iraq, the U.S. and other NATO countries supported the Iraqi chemical and biological weapons programs in addition to providing intelligence, arms, and money.

At the outset of the war, Iraq used riot control methods in order to secure a fast and easy victory. As the war turned in Iran's favor, Hussein began ordering the use of chemical weapons against Iranian troops in hopes of reversing Iraqi territorial losses. In mid-1983, Iraqi troops began to use mustard gas and in 1984, Iraq was the first country to use a nerve agent on the battlefield when it deployed tabun-filled aerial bombs on enemy troops. By 1986, it was estimated that Iraqi chemical warfare was responsible for more than 10,000 casualties. The most lethal doses of chemical and nerve agents, though, were reserved for the Kurds in the north.

Kurdish rebellions were especially problematic in the 1980s while Iraq was engaged in military action against Iran. Iraqi troops stationed in the northern part of the country were being killed by Kurdish rebels as they left their camps for food and water, and some Kurds openly aided Iran. In retaliation, Hussein designed a gruesome punishment for the insurgents.

Testing the effects of various chemical and biological agents, Hussein's infamous cousin **Ali Hassan Majid** (aka "**Chemical Ali**") dumped typhoid spores into Kurdish water supplies in 1987, killing hundreds of people. Later, he used gas attacks to take the lives of another hundred Kurdish villagers. But the most disturbing attack took place in March 1988 against the Kurds living in the border town of **Halabja**. (see Kurds pg. 63)

Canisters filled with the nerve gases tabun, sarin and soman as well as mustard gas were strategically dropped around the village, causing thousands of Kurdish men, women and children to die almost instantly. The rebellions stopped immediately. It is for these crimes against humanity that Hussein and his cohorts were tried, condemned and executed by Iraqi authorities in 2006.

Emboldened by his success, Hussein unleashed another round of chemi-

Iraq in a Nutshell

cal attacks on Iranian forces. After eight years of war, the Ayatollah Khomeini was finally compelled to sue for peace.

During the Gulf War, Hussein had ordered his military to fire chemical weapons on coalition troops if they reached Baghdad. But when the coalition stopped short of the capital (and in light of U.S. threats of retaliation with nuclear weapons), they held their fire. Although there is still no evidence that unconventional weapons were used against coalition forces in the 1990s, reports from Gulf War soldiers complaining of respiratory problems, fatigue, skin rashes, headaches, intestinal problems and other ailments (collectively called "**Gulf War Syndrome**") have led to suspicions that some foul play had occurred.

After years of post-war inspections (per **Resolution 687**) and the consequent destruction of stockpiles of chemical weapons and the facilities that produced them, the West believed that Hussein still had the ability to re-establish its chemical warfare program at any time. Experts said it was possible that Iraq concealed several dozen warheads that could be filled with chemical or biological weapons and launched at Israel, Saudi Arabia or other neighboring nations. The Bush administration claimed that the country had caches of deadly chemicals at its disposal and that production of chemical and biological agents could easily be undertaken in "dual-use" facilities (buildings for industrial and commercial use that could be quickly converted for military use), or even portable laboratories, without detection. This claim was used as justification to pass **UN Resolution 1441** which called on Iraq to prove that it didn't possess WMDs. When Iraq submitted insufficient evidence, the U.S. invaded Iraq.

After invasion, U.S. troops searched the country and found no evidence of Iraqi WMDs.

Iraq in a Nutshell

UN RESOLUTIONS
THE ROAD TO WAR

660 (Adopted August 2, 1990)
　　Condemns the Iraqi invasion of Kuwait. Demands that Iraq withdraw immediately and unconditionally all of its forces back to the position held on August 1, 1990.

661 (August 6, 1990)
　　Determines that Iraq has failed to comply with Resolution 660. Decides that no countries shall import any commodities or products originating in Iraq or Kuwait.

687 (April 3, 1991)
　　Declares a formal cease-fire between Iraq, Kuwait and the coalition forces.
　　Demands the restoration of friendly relations between Iraq and Kuwait.
　　Decides that Iraq shall destroy or remove all chemical and biological weapons and all related components and research related to the development of such weapons as well as ballistic missiles with a range greater than 150 kilometers (shorter than the distance from Iraq to Israel).
　　Decides that Iraq shall submit a declaration of the locations, amounts and types of items specified above and agrees to on-site inspections.
　　Decides that a Special Commission will be formed to carry out immediate on-site inspection of Iraq's biological, chemical and missile capabilities, based on Iraq's declarations.
　　Decides that Iraq shall unconditionally agree not to acquire or develop nuclear weapons or nuclear-weapons-usable material or any subsystems or components or any research, development, support or manufacturing facilities related to the above.
　　Decides that Iraq shall return all Kuwaiti property seized by Iraq, including a list of any property that Kuwait claims has not been returned or which has not been returned intact.
　　Decides that all Iraqi statements repudiating its foreign debt are null and void and demands that Iraq adhere scrupulously to all its obligations concerning servicing and repayment of its foreign debt.
　　Decides that the embargo shall not apply to foodstuffs nor to materials and supplies essential to civilian needs.

Iraq in a Nutshell

Decides that the economic embargo will be lifted if Iraq complies with the resolutions outlined above.

Requires Iraq to declare that it will not commit or support any act of international terrorism or allow any organization directed towards commission of such acts to operate within its territory.

688 (April 5, 1991)

Condemns the repression of the Iraqi civilian population in many parts of Iraq, including in Kurdish populated areas.

699 (June 17, 1991)

Confirms that the Special Commission and the IAEA have the authority to conduct activities under resolution 687 (1991), for the purpose of supervising the destruction, removal or rendering harmless of the items specified in that resolution.

706 (August 15, 1991)

(Oil-for-food) Permits all countries to import petroleum and petroleum products from Iraq. Decides that payment for petroleum products will be put into an escrow account to be administered by the Secretary-General of the UN and used for the purchase of foodstuffs, medicines and materials and supplies for essential civilian needs and to pay for costs incurred by the UN in facilitating the return of all Kuwaiti property seized by Iraq.

986 (April 14, 1995)

Expands the "oil-for-food" exceptions to the trade embargo and authorizes Turkey to import petroleum and petroleum products from Iraq through the Kirkuk-Yumurtalik pipeline as long as it does not exceed prescribed limits and complies with terms outlined in resolution 706.

1060 (June 12, 1996)

Deplores the refusal of the Iraqi authorities to allow access to sites by UNSCOP in a clear violation of the provisions of Security Council resolution 687.

1134 (October 23, 1997)

Condemns the repeated refusal of the Iraqi authorities to allow access to certain sites by UNSCOM in violation of resolution 687.

1137 (November 12, 1997)

Condemns Iraqi restrictions on access by UNSCOM.

Iraq in a Nutshell

1194 (September 9, 1998)
Condemns Iraq's lack of cooperation with the Special Commission and IAEA.

1205 (November 5, 1998)
Condemns the decision made by Iraq on October 31, 1998 to cease cooperation with the Special Commission as a flagrant violation of resolution 687 (1991) and other relevant resolutions.

1284 (December 17, 1999)
Establishes, as a subsidiary body of the Council, the United Nations Monitoring, Verification and Inspection Commission (UNMOVIC) – to replace UNSCOM.

1441 (November 8, 2002)
Declares Iraq in material breach of its obligations under past resolutions (in particular 687) through Iraq's failure to cooperate with UN inspectors and the IAEA.

Decides to offer Iraq a final opportunity to comply with disarmament obligations. Iraq shall provide to UNMOVIC and IAEA and Council no later than 30 days from date of the resolution complete declaration of all aspects of its programs to develop chemical, biological and nuclear weapons, ballistic missiles and other delivery systems.

The resolution also "recalls that Iraq has been warned that it will face serious consequences if it continues to violate its obligations."

SPAIN, U.K., NORTHERN IRELAND AND US PROVISIONAL RESOLUTION (March 7, 2003)
Not passed (see box Votes for War Resolution pg. 45)
Reaffirms the need for full implementation of resolution 1441. Decides that Iraq will have failed to take the final opportunity afforded by resolution 1441 unless on, or before March 17, 2003, the Council concludes that Iraq has demonstrated full, unconditional, immediate and active cooperation in accordance with its disarmament obligations under Resolution 1441 and is yielding to UNMOVIC and IAEA of all weapons, weapon delivery and support systems and structures prohibited by resolution 687.

1483 (May 22, 2003)
Declares an end of sanctions, in force since 1990, and recognizes Britain and the US as occupying powers ("The Authority") calling on them to improve security and stability.

Iraq in a Nutshell

IRAQ STUDY GROUP REPORT

In March 2006, the U.S. Congress appointed a bipartisan panel to assess the situation in Iraq and make policy recommendations. The panel, called the Baker-Hamilton Commission after its co-chairs, former Secretary of State James Baker III and former U.S. Representative Lee Hamilton, released the Iraq Study Group Report: The Way Forward – A New Approach, nine months later.

Among 79 recommended changes in policy were *(excerpts)*:

Recommendation 1: "The U.S., working with the Iraqi government, should launch a comprehensive New Diplomatic Offensive to deal with the problems of Iraq and of the region."

Recommendation 2: i) Support the unity and territorial integrity of Iraq; iii) secure Iraq's borders; ix) help Iraq reach a mutually acceptable agreement on Kirkuk; x) help the Iraqi government meet security, political and economic milestones (including national reconciliation, equitable distribution of oil revenues and dismantling of militias); and v) promote trade, economic assistance and, if possible, military assistance to Iraq's government from non-neighboring Muslim nations.

Recommendation 5: An international Support Group should be created including Iraq and all the states bordering Iraq including Iran, Syria, Egypt and the Gulf States, the five permanent members of the UN Security Council and the European Union.

Recommendation 9-12 (*Iran and Syria*): Under the aegis of the New Diplomatic Offensive and the Support Group, the U.S. should engage directly with Iran and Syria in order to try to obtain their commitment to constructive policies towards Iraq, and other regional issues.

(The suggestion to engage Syria and Iran [a member of G.W. Bush's "Axis of Evil"] to help end violence and rebuild Iraq was particularly controversial)

Recommendation 13-16 (Israel-Palestine): There must be a renewed and sustained commitment by the U.S. to a comprehensive Arab-Israeli peace on all fronts.

(Iraqi critics objected to what they considered misdirected

linkage of the Arab-Israeli conflict with Iraq. They also felt the Report put America's interests ahead of Iraq's and deemed it a threat to Iraq's sovereignty)

Recommendation 19-25 (*Milestones*): The U.S. President must stay in close contact with the Iraqi leadership and encourage the Iraqi government to make substantial progress toward the achievement of milestones. If the Iraqi government does not make substantial progress toward the achievement of milestones on national reconciliation, security and government the U.S. should reduce its political, military or economic support for the Iraqi government. As Iraq becomes more capable of governing, defending and sustaining itself, the U.S. military and civilian presence in Iraq can be reduced.

(Among the milestones: approval of petroleum (oil-revenue sharing), de-Baathification and militia laws by early 2007; a referendum on constitutional amendments by March 2007; provincial elections by June 2007; Iraqi increase of security spending, Iraqi control of the Iraqi army by April 2007; Iraqi control of provinces by September 2007; and Iraqi security self-reliance by December 2007.)

Recommendation 30: International arbitration is necessary to avert violence in Kirkuk.

Recommendation 32: The rights of women and all minority communities must be protected.

Recommendation 40: The United States should not make an open-ended commitment to keep large numbers of American troops deployed in Iraq.

(The Committee gave three reasons for American withdrawal: first, a continued commitment of American troops in Iraq would leave too few ground forces to deal with other emergencies [for instance, action against Iran or North Korea if needed]; second, long-term deployment of troops in Iraq has left less than 1/3 of the Army ready to be deployed elsewhere; and third, an open-ended commitment of American forces would not provide the Iraqi government the incentive it needs to take the political actions necessary to quell the violence.

Neocons and other critics of the Iraq Study Group Report

have accused the authors of misguidedly advocating American surrender to the terrorists.)

Recommendation 41-45: The Iraqi government should assume responsibility for Iraqi security by increasing the size and capabilities of the Iraqi Army. While this process is underway, the U.S. should increase the number of U.S. military personnel by 10,000 to 20,000 American troops to help train and advise the Iraqi forces.

Recommendation 50-61: The Iraqi national Police Service, Border Police and Ministry of the Interior should be overhauled with help from U.S. specialists.

Recommendation 62-63 (*Oil*): The U.S. government should help the Iraqi government prepare oil laws, protect oil infrastructure and contractors, improve pipeline security, reorganize the national oil industry, improve accountability in the oil sector and combat corruption.

Recommendation 64-65 (*Reconstruction*): The U.S. should increase economic assistance to Iraq and actively participate in the country's reconstruction including assistance with job creation and providing essential government services (trash pickup, water, sewers and electricity).

Recommendation 72 (*Cost of war*): Costs for the war in Iraq should be included in the President's Annual Budget request. Funding requests for the war in Iraq should be presented clearly to Congress and the American people.

****

Other books by Amanda Roraback

IRAN in a Nutshell
AFGHANISTAN in a Nutshell
ISLAM in a Nutshell
PAKISTAN in a Nutshell
ISRAEL-PALESTINE in a Nutshell
CHINA in a Nutshell

For more information about Enisen Publishing please visit www.enisen.com.